Jotham's Journey

Jotham's Journey

A Storybook for Advent

ARNOLD YTREEIDE

SERVANT PUBLICATIONS
ANN ARBOR, MICHIGAN

Vine Books is an imprint of Servant Publications especially designed to serve evangelical Christians.

All Scripture quotations, unless indicated, are taken from the HOLY BIBLE, NEW INTERNATIONAL VERSION®. © 1973, 1978, 1984, by International Bible Society. Used by permission of Zondervan Publishing House. All rights reserved.

Published by Servant Publications
P.O. Box 8617
Ann Arbor, Michigan 48107

Cover design and illustrations: Hile Illustration and Design, Ann Arbor, Michigan

Printed in the United States of America
ISBN 1-56955-020-4 (hardcover edition)
ISBN 1-56955-202-9 (paper edition)

LIBRARY OF CONGRESS CATALOGING-IN-PUBLICATION DATA

Ytreeide, Arnold.
Jotham's journey : a storybook for Advent / Arnold Ytreeide.
     p.   cm.
ISBN 1-56955-020-4
1. Advent—Prayer-books and devotions—English.   2. Family—Prayer-books and devotions—English.   I. Title.
BV40.Y77   1997   97-7889
242'.332—dc21   CIP

For Jonathan and Jessica
My Children

A Story for Advent

"Stir us up, O Lord, to make ready for your only-begotten Son. May we be able to serve you with purity of soul through the coming of him who lives and reigns."

Advent Prayer

Advent. *Adventus. Ecce advenit Dominator Dominus.* Behold, the Lord, the Ruler, is come. Reaching back two millennia to the birth of the Christ child and forward to his reign on earth, the tradition of Advent is a threefold celebration of the birth of Jesus, his eventual second coming to earth, and his continued presence in our lives here and now. God in our past, God in our future, God in our present.

Advent.

It started with people going hungry to purify and prepare themselves for holy living. A *fast*, we call it, and such a fast was ordered by the Council of Saragossa in A.D. 381. For three weeks before Epiphany (a feast in January that commemorates the divine revelation of Jesus to the gentile Magi), the people were to prepare themselves by fasting and prayer. The tradition spread to France in A.D. 581 by decree of the Council of Macon, and to Rome and beyond thereafter. Gregory the First refined the season to its present form in about 600 when he declared that it should start the fourth Sunday before Christmas.

Fasting is no longer a part of Advent in most homes and churches (though it wouldn't be a bad idea). For us it means taking a few minutes each day, for the three or four weeks before Christmas, to center our thoughts on Truth Incarnate lying in a feeding trough in Bethlehem. It's a time of worship, a time of reflection, a time of focus, and a time of family communion. In the midst of December's commotion and stress, Advent is a few moments to stop, catch your breath, and renew your strength from the only One who can provide true strength.

Jotham's Journey is one tool you can use to implement a time of Advent in your family—whether yours is a traditional family structure, or one of the many combinations of fathers and mothers, step-parents and grandparents and guardians and children that make up today's families. You can use this story during Advent even if your family is just you.

Set aside a few minutes each day, beginning the fourth Sunday before Christmas (see the chart in the back of the book) to light the Advent candles, read the *Jotham* story and devotional for that day, and pray together. You can also use an Advent calendar (see sidebar), sing a favorite Christ-centered carol (Frosty's a nice guy, but has no place in Advent), and have a time of family sharing.

In our family, we set aside fifteen minutes each night before the youngest child goes to bed. Our Advent wreath has a traditional place on a table next to the living room reading chair. The children take turns lighting the candles and reading all the windows of the Advent calendar, and then adding that day's reading at the end. By the light of the Advent candles I read the last few lines of the previous day's Jotham story, then go on to today's story and devotion. Afterwards my wife leads in prayer as we all hold hands. We close by singing one verse of a carol. Then the youngest child lights her own "bedside" candle from the Advent candles and makes her way to bed by candlelight. (This is only for children who are old enough to know how to use a candle safely.) Even when work or visiting takes us out of town, we carry *Jotham* and a candle with us to keep our Advent tradition. Sometimes we even get to share our tradition with those we are visiting.

Simple, short, spiritual. A wonderful way to keep the shopping, traffic, rehearsals, concerts, parties, and all the other preparations of December in balance with the reality of God in our lives—past, present, and future.

Advent. *Adventus. Ecce advenit Dominator Dominus.* Behold, the Lord, the Ruler, is come. May God richly bless you and your family as you prepare to celebrate the birth of Christ!

Advent Customs

Advent itself is simply any time set apart for spiritual preparation. But most people associate the word Advent with various traditions and customs that have grown up around Christmas in many of the world's cultures. Early in history these customs took the forms of fasts and feasts. Today, they most often take the form of candles, wreaths, and calendars.

Most churches and families use Advent candles to celebrate the season. One candle is used for each week of Advent and a fifth for Christmas Day. The first, second, and fourth candles are violet, symbolizing penitence. The third is pink, symbolizing joy, and the Christmas Day candle is white, symbolizing the purity of Christ.

Advent candles are usually part of an Advent wreath. While some traditions hang the wreath, it is most commonly used flat, on a table. The circle of the wreath represents the hope of eternal life we have through Christ. The circle itself is made of evergreen branches, symbolizing the abundant life Jesus promised us here and now. The first four candles are positioned along the outside ring of the wreath and the fifth is placed in the center.

Some traditions use a slanted board instead of a wreath to hold the candles. The board is about four inches by twelve, and raised six inches on one end. Four holes are drilled along the length of the board for the first four candles, and the fifth candle is placed at the top.

Advent calendars are popular with children and teach them the Christmas story in an active way. Also called an "Advent house," the calendar is shaped like a house, with a window for each day of Advent. Behind each window is a small portion of the Christmas story (usually from the Book of Luke). Each night the family reads the story from these windows, ending with the window for that day.

Darkness

Light the first violet candle.

Jotham pulled the scratchy grey blanket more tightly around his shoulders, but the wind still slithered down his neck. It was colder now that the sun had dropped below the bare hilltops behind him. Far off to his right was the salty sea where nothing lived. And just over that ridge in front of him—the one that formed the other side of the valley he was in—his family camped. They would be asleep now, warm and safe inside the finest goatskin tents ever made. *I would be, too,* Jotham thought. *If only Father weren't so stubborn!*

A devil's howl came from somewhere in the distance and echoed off the valley walls. A jackal, Jotham knew instantly. A wild dog. Far enough away as not to be a danger to his little herd of lambs, though on this particular night he had no lambs to worry about. Still, the sound stabbed at Jotham's heart like a knife. He sat perfectly still for several minutes, careful not to make even a breath of noise. One couldn't be too cautious when jackals were about.

The jackal howled again. Closer this time, Jotham judged. The thought sent tingles spreading out from his spine, like a million ants biting his skin. Not that he was afraid, of course. He was Jotham of Jericho, after all! Ready to fight jackals or snakes or bears to defend his flock!

But, still, a ten-year-old boy, alone, with only his tunic, his staff, and a little wool blanket, could be a very tempting meal for a hungry jackal. Jotham wedged himself a little deeper into the craggy rock. He didn't really like the thought of spending another night in the cold, but it was worth it, wasn't it? Jotham wasn't quite so sure anymore.

Everything had been fine until yesterday. Each morning Jotham would gather his lambs, lead them to the drinking hole, and then to a small field of green grass where they could eat and play all day. In the evening he'd bring them back to camp again, to rejoin the rest of the flock. His older brothers would do the same with the bigger sheep, only his *brothers* got to go to the fields that were bigger and farther away. Sometimes they even got to spend a whole night out with their flock, sleeping under the stars on goatskin mats Mother had made for them. They even got to take their meals with them, carrying them in special baskets that stacked on top of each other and tied together with a leather thong. All *Jotham* ever got was a piece of bread and a chunk of dried meat, carried in a bag made from the stomach of a goat. A bag that was now empty, Jotham remembered, and his stomach let out a growl so loud he was afraid the jackal would hear.

But then yesterday everything had changed. Jotham had just picked up his lunch bag and hugged his mother when he heard his father talking to Jethro, Ephraim, and Eleazar, his older brothers. "Take your flocks to the Valley of Hebron," his father was saying. "You will find there a man named Zadok of Kadesh. Sell him the better tenth of your sheep. He will give you a fair price."

At those words Jotham's heart began to ache. The Valley of Hebron! That was right next to the *city* of Hebron! His brothers were going to a city with thousands of people, a marketplace full of exotic foods and magical toys, a city with deep wells and brightly colored flags and music that played all day and all night. Hebron! Oh how Jotham longed to go with his brothers, to see the sights and to smell the smells of a city of wonders. In fact he could almost taste …

"I'm going with them!"

The sound of Jotham's voice had shocked even himself. At his words everyone stopped, then turned and stared at him. Finally, his father spoke.

"This task is for your brothers, Jotham. You are not yet ready to leave your mother's side."

"I'm going with them!" Jotham had said again, his voice so loud and high that the sheep near-by began to wail in fright. "It's not fair that they get to go to Hebron and I have to stay here."

Jotham's father took a deep breath, then walked slowly toward him. Jotham tried to keep the fear he felt from showing on his face. His father was a big man, tall as a tree, it seemed. And strong. Jotham had once seen him wrestle a full-sized camel to the ground when it went mad from disease.

But instead of raising his hand or his voice to Jotham, his father slowly knelt down on one knee to look at him eye-to-eye, and placed his hand gently on Jotham's shoulder. "Jotham," he said evenly, "your time for journeys away from my tent will come soon, but it is not yet here. You will remain with me and tend to your lambs."

Jotham fought to hold back the anger and the tears. He knew the sting of his father's hand, and did not wish to know it again, but this was so unfair!

"I want to go," he said, lips trembling.

"Yes, I know," his father answered. "But you cannot. There are too many dangers, and your brothers have enough responsibilities without looking after you as well."

Jotham wanted to yell at his father, to say awful things that would make his father hurt as much as *he* did. But he dared not. So instead he pushed aside his father's hand and turned and ran away. He ran to the water hole, and then beyond it. He ran over the hills where he grazed his lambs, then over the other side until he could no longer see the tents of his father. And then he kept running. When he finally stopped, he sat down at the base of a gnarled tree and cried out his anger and frustration. "You can't tell *me* what to do," he yelled into the wind. And he decided then and there that he would not go back to his father's tent until his father could treat him like a man!

And so he had sat in the shade, waiting for nothing except time to pass, and thinking angry thoughts about his father and brothers. When the sun was directly overhead, he took out the bread and meat his mother had packed. He ate it all in the time it took for an ant to carry a single crumb to its nest a few feet away. After that he had started to walk among the rocks and cliffs and canyons, places he had never seen before. He practiced throwing rocks with his leather sling, and drew pictures in the dirt with a stick. And slowly, as his anger began to disappear, he became afraid. Not of bears or snakes or scorpions, but afraid of what he had done.

Late in the afternoon he began to hear his brothers and father far off in the distance calling his name. He wanted to answer, but he just couldn't bring himself to apologize. The voices continued throughout the evening, and each time he heard his name, another measure of guilt was sprinkled on his heart. But he *could not* answer! They would all laugh at him, and tell stories of his foolishness. And so he kept quiet.

Just before the sun had dropped completely behind the cliffs, the voices had stopped. No one called his name any longer. The air became cold and damp, and Jotham longed to return to the fires of his father's tent. But then he thought of his brothers. They were on their way to Hebron by now, and this made Jotham angry all over again. *Let them make their journey,* he decided. *I'll stay here and let Father worry! I'll show him I'm big enough to take care of myself!*

But the night was long and held very little sleep for Jotham. When the sun finally peeked over the ridge to the east and began to calm the shivers that had shaken his body all night, he ached to feel his mother's hug and taste her morning stew. There was no anger in him any longer, only fear. He felt fear of the punishment he was sure to receive.

And so he had devised a plan. He would cross back over the great ridge and move closer to his father's tents, to the field where the lambs graze. His father would be sure to find him there. With a rock, Jotham would scrape his forehead until it bled, making it look as if he'd been attacked by thieves. He'd even throw his lunch bag and staff away to make his story seem true. Then he would lie there and pretend to be unconscious until his father came and found him. His father would have sympathy for Jotham, and maybe punish him a bit less.

Immediately, Jotham jumped to his feet to carry out his plan. It took most the following morning to find his grazing field—everything looked so strange from this side of the ridge. Once there, he found a hand-size stone. But it was much harder to make the injury than he had imagined. The rough rock hitting his forehead really hurt! He finally managed to draw a little blood. Then he lay down to wait. And wait. And wait.

But nobody ever came.

As the sun began to set again Jotham became angry once more. *They didn't even care enough to come and look for me,* he thought. *Well, I'll show them! I'll just stay out here and let them worry!*

And so here he was now, pulling the scratchy grey blanket more tightly around his shoulders, his stomach grumbling and aching as it never had before, and listening to a jackal howl in the distance. *Maybe I should just go back,* Jotham thought now. *There's food in my father's tent. All the punishment in the world would be worth it if I could have even a bite of bread.*

The jackal wailed once more, much closer now. *Maybe father was right,* Jotham thought. *It is dangerous out here. And I could probably never keep up with my brothers on the long trip to Hebron, they're so much bigger and stronger.*

Suddenly Jotham made a decision. He jumped to his feet, pulled the blanket around himself, and headed off across the valley toward his father's tents, watching his step in the moonlight. *I will tell Father I was wrong,* he decided, *and ask his forgiveness. I will take my punishment, and then I will eat. Yes, I will eat!* The thought of his mother's bread and a thick slice of meat made Jotham's mouth water. *I will eat and I will sleep by the fire, and tomorrow I will take my lambs to graze just like always.*

As Jotham neared the watering hole he actually began to smile, glad that his little journey was finally over. But then he came around the last of the hills … and stopped dead in his tracks.

His father's tents were gone.

The broad field where they had camped was now bare. The fire pits were cold. The sheep pens were empty.

They left me! Jotham thought. *They didn't even care enough to come and look for me!* He sat in the dirt and began to cry, and he cried for what seemed like most of the night. He cried at the thought of being alone, he cried at the thought of being left behind. But mostly, he cried at the thought that his father didn't love him enough to stay and look for him. He felt as if some rough, giant hand was crushing his heart between its fingers.

Finally, still sobbing, Jotham stood and began to pick through the remains of the camp, hoping to find a corner of bread or a scrap of meat. His stomach ached as much as his heart, and he felt as empty and alone as a newborn lamb that has been separated from its mother.

Finding no food or any trace of his family, Jotham slowly walked back to the watering hole. At least he could fill his stomach with water, he thought. Maybe it would make some of the pain go away. But, just as he knelt to lap up the water, he noticed a pile of stones, just off the path that led to the lambs' grazing field. Curious, he walked over and examined the pile in the moonlight. The ground around the stones was darker, and a funny smell hung in the air.

It was blood, he suddenly realized. And then he saw it. Blood. Everywhere. And bits of fur and flesh and, leading off into the bushes, scuff marks, as if something had been dragged away.

Then he noticed that there was writing on the top stone in the pile, something scratched into its flat surface. Jotham could not read very much, only a few words that had to do with the keeping of sheep. But there was one word that Jotham *could* read, and he gasped as he saw it now, written on that stone topping the pile.

It was his name.

"Jotham," it said. What the other words said he did not know, but this one word was clear. And so was its meaning, on top of stones piled like this.

"They think I'm dead!" Jotham wailed out loud. "They think I was killed by some animal and dragged off to be eaten!" And then he began to cry again, not a cry of anger anymore, and not a cry of loneliness. A cry of fear.

"I want my father," he cried, and fell with his face in the dirt, clutching his little blanket. "I want my father!" he screamed over and over. But there was no one there to hear him. Finally, after a very long time, he realized that his family wouldn't even be looking for him. It was *he* who would have to find *them*. But where would he look? Which way did they go? How long had they been gone?

Jotham didn't know, but he knew he must search. He lay there next to the pile of stones that marked the place where his family thought he'd been killed, the scratchy grey blanket pulled tightly around himself, his face buried in the dirt, his crying turned to quick, stabbing sobs. *I must look for my family. I must search until I find them, wherever they are,* he thought.

And somewhere, very close by, a jackal howled.

For centuries, the people of Israel rebelled against God.

He had called them his chosen people. They called *him* cruel and unfair.

He had given them a land flowing with milk and honey. They thanked and worshipped *other* gods.

So finally, 750 years before Jesus was born, God sent the prophet Isaiah to the children of Israel. Through Isaiah, God said to them:

> Hear, O heavens! Listen, O earth! For the Lord has spoken: "I reared children and brought them up, but they have rebelled against me.... " Ah, sinful nation, a people loaded with guilt, a brood of evildoers, children given to corruption! They have forsaken the Lord; they have spurned the Holy One of Israel and turned their backs on him. ISAIAH 1:2-4

But God didn't send Isaiah just to condemn the people of Israel. He also sent him to explain that it didn't have to be that way. He sent Isaiah to give them a message of hope, if only they would listen:

> "Come now, let us reason together," says the Lord. "Though your sins are like scarlet, they shall be as white as snow; though they are red as crimson, they shall be like wool. If you are willing and obedient, you will eat the best from the land; but if you resist and rebel, you will be devoured by the sword." ISAIAH 1:18-20

And then Isaiah told Israel a great secret, a secret of one who was coming that would save them from the darkness they had created for themselves:

The people walking in darkness have seen a great light.... For to us a child is born, to us a son is given, and the government will be upon his shoulders. And he will be called Wonderful Counselor, Mighty God, Everlasting Father, Prince of Peace.   ISAIAH 9:2, 6, 7

Today we begin the Advent season by lighting the first violet candle. This candle reminds us of God's promise that, though like Israel we have been disobedient children who are lost and alone in the desert, he has sent a Messiah, a shining light, a Savior, to lead us back to God.

Like Jotham, we each have a long journey ahead of us—a journey that unfolds day by day. But, also like Jotham, we can be confident that no matter what we encounter along the way, we can have hope and faith in a God who loves us, and who desires only the best for us.

If only we'll seek him.

First Light

Light the first violet candle.

The jackal bared his teeth and growled low and evil. His eyes glowed red in the firelight. He stood as tall as Jotham, and his splotchy black fur hung on his bony frame like moss on a dead tree. The beast was starving and had just found food.

Jotham's chest heaved with every terrified beat of his heart. He wanted to scream, but all his screams were caught inside his throat. *Run!* he kept thinking to himself. But his legs refused.

The jackal leaped through the air! Now Jotham turned to run, but it was too late. He had gone only a single step when a red-hot iron clamped around his right leg and knocked him crashing into the ground. Fire exploded in every nerve and finally he screamed.

Claws dug into his bare leg now, and then the jaw clamped down once more. Jotham fought to roll onto his back, then kicked at the bloody face. But the demon was stronger, and pinned Jotham to the ground with three hundred pounds of muscle.

Bared teeth hovered over Jotham's face now, and he saw his own blood dripping from their needle-like points. The stench of breath and fur filled Jotham's nose, but he didn't have time to care. Because now the jackal let out one great, long victory howl, and then plunged his teeth deep into Jotham's throat.

"Ow!"

Jotham sat bolt upright, slapping at the sting on his neck. He blinked rapidly in the harsh sunlight, and his eyes watered in pain. He pulled his hand away from his neck and through blurry eyes saw the smashed remains of a wasp lying in his palm.

It was all a dream, Jotham laughed to himself. His heart was beating fast, he was breathing in giant gasps, but it had only been a dream. *There was no jackal, no fight with his father, no lost family.*

Still groggy, Jotham pulled himself to his feet and brushed off the dirt. *Why was I lying next to the water hole?* he wondered. *And why was I asleep in the dirt in the middle of the day?*

Then he saw the pile of stones and in one awful rush of reality, he knew.

It *hadn't* all been a dream. The jackal had never attacked, that was true. But he really was alone. He really was lost. He really was … *hungry!*

Jotham wandered through the bare campsite. In the daylight it wasn't nearly as frightening, but it *was* still deserted. He couldn't figure out why his parents had gone. Even if Jotham *had* been killed, that was no reason to move the whole camp. But something in the back of his brain kept gnawing at him. It seemed as if, a couple times in the last few weeks, he had heard his parents talk of moving the camp. He never paid attention to their conversations, of course. Adults talk about such dull things. But it seemed like there was some important thing they were concerned about. Some reason they had to move.

No matter, Jotham sighed. The fact was, they were gone and he was alone. Now *he* had to find *them,* since they didn't know he was alive and wouldn't be looking for him. But which way did they go? The camp had been built close to a main road. Where it came from and where it went Jotham had no idea, but many caravans passed by each month. He studied the tracks on the road for a long time trying to figure out which way his family had gone, but it was impossible. The winter wind had mixed all the tracks together. So now he had to make a decision: go left or go right?

No matter what he had told his father, Jotham hated making decisions, especially when there was just no way to know the right thing to do. Finally, he decided to go to his right, toward where the sun rose each morning. So after taking a long drink at the watering hole and tying his scratchy little blanket around his waist, he started walking.

Jotham liked walking on roads. Most shepherds liked to stay out in the hills, wandering from this place to that, not really caring where they were. But roads took you from one place to another place, and Jotham liked that. He liked having a specific purpose for his walking.

Of course, Jotham had no idea what specific place *this* road came from or went to. And he had no idea if he was *following* his family or walking *away* from them. He could only hope and pray.

He had only been walking about an hour when the pain in his stomach began to overpower him. I've got to find some food, he thought. But where? The sides of the road were bare and rocky. A few bushes pushed their way up through the rocks, but they were all brown and bare in the coolness of winter.

Suddenly Jotham forgot all about his aching stomach. He had just climbed a short hill when he saw that the road ahead of him entered a narrow canyon. Sharp rocks stuck out at all angles, creating dozens of places to hide. Jotham knew his father worried at places like this, and would always make the caravan move in close together. These were the kinds of places where robbers hid. Usually they'd leave a large caravan alone, but Jotham remembered one time when three men had attacked one of his uncles, stolen his purse, and vanished into the hills before anyone else could help.

So what chance does a ten-year-old boy have? Jotham thought.

By now the hunger had made Jotham's head feel like it was floating. The empty feeling went clear from the bottom of his feet to the top of his head, and there was an awful buzzing sound in his ears. As he got closer to the canyon his heart began to pound in his chest. He tried to look between the rocks ahead, searching for any sign of robbers, but couldn't quite get his eyes to focus. He passed from the sunlight into the shadows of the canyon, and the walls themselves seemed to be alive. It felt as if they were moving in closer with every step he took, moving in to crush him between their craggy fingers. Sounds seemed to echo off the walls: strange sounds, awful sounds, scary sounds.

Jotham tried to follow the sounds with his eyes, tried to look at every rock and crevice at once. He spun this way and that, imagining at every turn a thief jumping at him with knife drawn and a sneer on his lips.

"Jehovah, save me!" Jotham screamed, and his scream scared a flock of birds out of their hiding place. They flew past Jotham's head, and he swatted at them and screamed again. Then he turned toward the other end of the canyon and started running. He ran from the birds and from the robbers he'd imagined and from the evil canyon walls. He ran and he cried and he screamed. But just as he thought he was about to safety, when the end of the canyon was steps away, a man with a long black beard jumped out from behind the rocks and landed right in front of Jotham. Jotham screamed and tried to jump to the side, but he tripped and fell and struck his head on a rock.

And everything went black.

Jotham moaned and gently rubbed his head. His eyes fluttered open, and all he could see was the face of the man with the long black beard. Jotham tried to pull away, but the man held his arm tightly.

"There there, little one. Be at peace," he said softly. Seeing the smile on the man's face, Jotham calmed a little and stopped struggling. There was a bright glow around the man's head, and his face beamed with kindness.

"I heard you calling the name of Jehovah," he said gently. "And so I came."

"Hear my cry, O God; listen to my prayer. From the ends of the earth I call to you, I call as my heart grows faint; lead me to the rock that is higher than I. For you have been my refuge, a strong tower against the foe. I long to dwell in your tent forever and take refuge in the shelter of your wings" (Ps 61:1-4).

This was the prayer of the Israelites as they searched for God. They were tired of sinning, tired of being afraid. So finally they called on Jehovah to rescue them. He answered them through the prophet Isaiah:

"So do not fear, for I am with you; do not be dismayed, for I am your God. I will strengthen you and help you; I will uphold you with my righteous right hand.… For I am the Lord, your God, who takes hold of your right hand and says to you, Do not fear; I will help you" (Is 41:10, 13).

Sometimes the fears we have are imagined, and sometimes they are real. Sometimes we are caught in situations over which we have no control, and sometimes we cause those situations ourselves. But God's word to Israel and to us is always the same: "Do not fear; I will help you."

Jotham still has a long journey ahead of him. But when he saw the situation he was in and called to God for help, God answered. "I will help you," he said.

I will help you.

That promise is the hope we hold on to as we look toward Christmas.

Comfort Ye

Light the first violet candle.

Jotham stared through blurry eyes at the man in the long black beard. A halo shown around his head, and his face glowed with the warmth of a friendly heart. Jotham's head was spinning from his fall and from starvation, and he felt as if he were tumbling into a big, black hole in the ground. With the last of his strength he reached through the fog before his eyes and gently stroked the man's face.

"You're … you're an angel of the Lord," he croaked softly.

The man smiled broadly revealing his crooked yellow teeth and chuckled. "No, little one, I am no angel." Then he moved to the side to help Jotham sit up, and blinding sunlight slapped Jotham square in the face. He let out a little yelp and put his hand up to shade his eyes.

"The sun," he whispered hoarsely. "The sun made your hair glow like … "

"Shh, shh, I understand," the man said. "But you must rest. I will carry you back to our camp." And just before Jotham let himself fall into the deep black hole of sleep, he felt two powerful arms lift him gently off the ground.

Cool water trickled down Jotham's throat, then the smell of freshly baked bread filled his nostrils. When Jotham opened his eyes he saw the bread, held inches from his mouth. He snapped it up faster than a frog catches a fly. He nipped the finger of the man who held the bread—the man with the long black beard—and the man let out a screech.

"Careful, little one," he said, shaking his hand quickly to stop the pain. "I know you are hungry, but we have better things to eat than my finger!"

Jotham didn't even hear him. All he knew was the bread in his mouth, and he chewed it until he was sure he had tasted every delicious crumb. And then there was another piece of bread, and meat, and some water. And pomegranates! He hadn't seen a pomegranate for a month! He let its sweet juice run down his chin and leak from the corners of his mouth as he took huge bites.

When finally his belly began to fill, Jotham looked up at the people gathered around him. He hadn't even noticed them before, but now saw the faces of men and women and children, all huddled around, looking down at him. He didn't recognize a single face, but he knew immediately just who they were by the way they dressed.

"Shepherds," he said. "You're shepherds."

Long Beard smiled a smile that brought out the laugh-lines around his mouth and eyes. "That is true," he said. "And so, too, are you, if I be any judge."

"Yes, sir," Jotham said politely. "I am Jotham of Jericho, defender of the lambs of my father!"

"And I," said Long Beard, "am Eliakim, son of Abijah. And who is *your* father, Jotham of Jericho?"

"He is Asa, son of Jacob," Jotham said, drawing his shoulders up square and straight.

Eliakim frowned and stroked his beard. "Hmm, Asa son of Jacob. I believe I know that name." He thought for a moment, then shook his head. "Ah, well, if I have heard that name I have long forgotten where. But now tell me, why is Jotham of Jericho out on the highway all alone? Where is your caravan?"

And so Jotham told him everything. All about how he had gone off to kill a lion that was bothering the flocks, and how his parents had thought he'd been killed and so had left him behind. That the part about the lion wasn't exactly true made Jotham feel a bit guilty, but he couldn't quite bring himself to tell his new friends that he'd been left behind because of a temper tantrum.

The look on Eliakim's face showed some doubt about the lion hunting, but Jotham didn't notice and went on with his story. When finally he finished Eliakim said, "So, the great hunter kills a lion with his bare hands, then finds fear in the rocks of a canyon?"

Jotham felt the blood rise in his face, embarrassed that he'd been caught in his lie. "Uh, well, I was very hungry, and everything looked so strange … and I … I … "

Eliakim smiled again and patted Jotham's shoulder. "And you called on the name of Jehovah, which is when I came running to help and startled you."

Jotham lowered his head and nodded. "And now," Eliakim said, looking around, "you have new friends and, if you need it, a new family!"

Jotham raised his head again, a smile stretching from ear to ear.

Eliakim quickly introduced Jotham to the rest of his clan. Jotham didn't remember most of the names, but he did remember the name of Eliakim's daughter, Tabitha. She was about Jotham's age, maybe a little younger, and was the one who had brought him the pomegranates.

When the introductions were finished, Jotham finally got to ask the question that had been burning inside him. "Master Eliakim," he said, his eyebrows creased into a frown, "have you seen any other caravans since yesterday?"

Eliakim shook his head slowly. "Sadly, no, my friend. We have just come from the hills to the south, and had only just approached this road when we heard your yell."

Jotham's lip began to tremble. "I … I was just hoping … "

"Yes, I understand. But you are safe now, and I say again that we will help you to find your family. But even if that fails, you may stay with us as long as you wish."

Jotham spent the rest of the day becoming familiar with the camp. He helped water the lambs, collected firewood, and picked out a sleeping mat and blanket with the help of Tabitha. After supper the whole family—about twenty aunts and uncles and cousins—sat around the fire, just like Jotham's family always did. After stories of the day and a good bit of joking about, Eliakim cleared his throat, and everyone fell silent.

"It is written," he started without introduction, "that Jehovah shall send His Anointed One to bind up the brokenhearted, to comfort all who mourn, and provide for those who grieve. And so we wait. We wait for that Anointed One to appear; we wait for the Messiah to reveal himself to us. But this day," he continued, looking now toward Jotham, "this day Jehovah has brought us one who cannot wait. He has brought one whose heart is broken, one who mourns, and one who grieves. And so," Eliakim said, looking now at the other faces in the camp, the light of the fire dancing on his own, "we ourselves must be like the Messiah to this young one. Even as we wait for Jehovah's Anointed, we must act as he would. We must do what we must to bind the broken heart, comfort he who mourns, provide for him who grieves. It is thus so, and it shall be, in the name of Jehovah."

As one, all those gathered around the fire said, "Selah," and it felt almost as good to Jotham as a hug from his mother. He truly did feel comforted, and his heart did ache a bit less this night. But still, as Eliakim continued to talk of the coming Messiah, Jotham's thoughts drifted back to his family. He wondered where they would be, he wondered where they were going, he wondered how much pain he had caused them.

And he was still wondering later that night, as he lay on his sleeping mat on the ground in front of Eliakim's tent. He gazed into the sky and let his mind wander and wonder among the stars. Just before he fell asleep he noticed one star that was just a bit brighter than the rest, and he wondered if, maybe, somewhere, his mother was looking at that very same star.

The people of Israel had to wait many centuries before the promised Messiah appeared. In the meantime, God comforted them with the words of the prophets, words of hope and promise. Words such as those recorded by Isaiah:

The Spirit of the Sovereign Lord is on me, because the LORD has anointed me to preach the good news to the poor. He has sent me to bind up the brokenhearted, to proclaim freedom for the captives and release from darkness for the prisoners, to proclaim the year of the Lord's favor and the day of vengeance of our God, to comfort all who mourn, and provide for those who grieve in Zion—to bestow on them a crown of beauty instead of ashes, the oil of gladness instead of mourning, and a garment of praise instead of a spirit of despair.   ISAIAH 61:1-3

These words were a comfort to the Israelites as they waited for the Messiah's coming, and they are a comfort to us today as we wait for his *second* coming. Because, even though we may face heartache and mourning and grief in this life, we can find comfort and healing through his presence in our lives today and the hope of a new heaven and new earth in the future.

Jotham has found kindness and love with the family of Eliakim, and it has eased the pain he feels at being separated from his family. But still, he looks forward to the day he will once again see the faces of his family, just as we look forward to the day we will see Jesus face-to-face.

Come quickly, Lord Jesus.

Family Ties

Light the first violet candle.

Jotham stretched and yawned, then rubbed his eyes. He had slept well this night, thanks to the kindness of Eliakim and his family. He took a deep breath to clear the night air from his lungs, then took a long look across the horizon. The sun was just rising above the barren hills to the east. Across the sky, in the west, still showing through the blue daylight, was the star he'd fallen asleep watching. Jotham didn't remember ever seeing a star in the daytime before. Maybe that's the Morning Star Mother and Father talk about, he thought.

Eliakim's family was up and working. His sons, all much older than Jotham, had already taken their sheep out to graze. Tabitha and her mother were busy making a stew for the midday meal when Jotham walked up.

"Good morning, Jotham of Jericho," Tabitha's mother said.

"Good morning, wife of Eliakim."

"Has your long sleep made you well?" she asked.

"Yes, I feel much better today."

Tabitha had sat there giggling through all this, and now her mother scolded her. "Tabitha," she said. "What *are* you going on about!?"

Another giggle escaped Tabitha's lips, then she said, "Your forgiveness, Mother, but I couldn't help notice that our new friend has some strange clothes."

Her mother looked to where Tabitha was pointing, then she, too, began to giggle. Jotham felt the blood rise in his cheeks, and he suddenly became very hot with embarrassment. He tried not to show any interest, but turned his head slightly and, out of the corner of his eye, checked his clothing.

And then he saw what they were laughing at. Hanging from his belt and dragging behind him like some kind of strange shawl was a long, narrow cloth that stretched back for more than twenty paces. "I … I …," Jotham stuttered, pulling at the cloth, but Tabitha and her mother just laughed.

"Forgive us, Jotham," the mother said, unhooking the cloth and rolling it up. "This is the swaddling cloth in which we wrap newborn babies. It must have been caught in the blanket we gave you." Then, seeing that he was still embarrassed, she added, "Tabitha, why don't you show Jotham your father's camp and tell him of your ancestors?"

"Yes, Mother," Tabitha said with the last of her giggles.

Tabitha led Jotham around the many tents of her father, explaining to him who lived in each and how they were all related. Family heritage was very important, Jotham knew, and he too had had to learn the names of relatives, many of whom he'd never met.

In between viewing tents and talk of family, Tabitha and Jotham spoke of many other things. Tabitha told him of the places they had traveled, and said that she had even been to Jericho once. Jotham beamed at this, proud that she had been to the place of his birth. He told her of the many wonders of Jericho, even though he'd only been there once himself.

"Are you the oldest of your brothers," Tabitha asked at one point.

"Uh, y … yes," Jotham stuttered. "I am the firstborn of my father!"

"You must be very proud," she said, then added, "and very sad at losing him."

Jotham hung his head in shame because of the truth he was hiding in his heart. "Yes, I am," was all he said.

That afternoon Eliakim called to Jotham to come and speak with him. "Tomorrow we will be leaving this place," he said, "and will travel west, to the city of my fathers."

Jotham frowned. The road he had been traveling ran east and west, and he was sure his family would be on it. After a moment he said, "Then I must part with you tomorrow. I must travel east, toward my family."

Now it was Eliakim who frowned. "I do not think that wise, little one. There are many dangers on the road, as you are fully aware. I think you should come with us. You really don't know that your family chose to travel east, or even if they are still on the road at all."

Jotham considered this for a few moments. He knew that Eliakim had the right to keep him there since he was so young and all alone. In fact, he was pretty sure that's what his parents would want. But the thought of traveling to the west while his family went east was almost more than he could bear. "Please, Eliakim! Allow me to search to the east. I'm sure my family is within a day's walk of this place!"

Eliakim sighed. He, too, knew that the law permitted him this decision, but he didn't know if he had the heart to keep a boy from his family. "I will consider it," he said finally, though he was pretty sure he knew what that decision would have to be.

After that, Jotham and Tabitha fetched water from a nearby stream and helped Tabitha's mother prepare the evening meal. It was while Jotham was pounding round dough into flat cakes that he first saw it.

"Caravan!" someone yelled, both in excitement at seeing another clan and in warning, in case it was not a *friendly* clan.

"I wonder who they are?" Tabitha said, jumping up to look. But Jotham didn't hear because he was already running. *This* caravan was coming up the road from the west!

By the time Jotham got to the front of the string of camels, the caravan had already stopped. Eliakim was talking to their leader, still seated on his camel and dressed in a long woolen robe of many colors. Running up, out of breath, Jotham looked up at the other leader and blurted out, "Have you seen my parents?"

Eliakim frowned at the interruption, but the caravan leader laughed. He had a kind face, Jotham thought, with a straight, black beard. He was tall, and his arms seemed as thick as a camel's neck. "And how would I know your parents?" the leader asked.

Ignoring Jotham, Eliakim took back the conversation that was clearly *his* to make as leader. He quickly explained the situation, and the other leader slowly shook his head.

"No, we have not seen such a caravan," he said. "And we have come all the way from Jerusalem."

Jotham grinned widely. Obviously this meant that he had been traveling the right direction, toward the east, since this new caravan would have passed his family if they had travelled west toward Jerusalem. Eliakim understood as well and let out a deep sigh. "I suppose this means you want to travel east, then," he said to Jotham.

Jotham just nodded rapidly, a grin lighting up his face. With an apologetic look, Eliakim turned back to the other leader. "Would you have room in your caravan for a small boy and a donkey?" he asked. At the mention of a donkey Jotham's mouth dropped open, and for a moment he was afraid that Eliakim thought he'd been hiding such an animal somewhere.

But the other leader smiled and said, "Of course, he may travel with us as far as he wishes." Eliakim turned to Jotham and said, "Tell Tabitha she is to give you the donkey her grandmother rode," and Jotham suddenly understood he was to receive a gift.

"I can never pay you or thank you enough for your kindness," Jotham said, repeating what he'd heard his father say on many occasions. Eliakim nodded his acceptance of the thanks, and then said, "It is in the name of Jehovah that I treat you thus. Now go quickly. These camels are restless."

Jotham ran his fastest back to the cook tent. There he found Tabitha and explained he was leaving, and what her father had said. The donkey that Tabitha led him to was old and looked like a worn-out Persian carpet, but Jotham didn't care. It was the animal that would take him to his family, and that made it the best animal in the world!

Quick goodbyes were said, and Tabitha's mother hastily packed some bread and meat for Jotham. But just as he was ready to climb onto the donkey, Jotham turned back to Tabitha.

"I … I'm not really the firstborn of my father," he said, his head hung in shame.

Tabitha just smiled. "I know," she said softly.

Jotham was pleased by her forgiving smile. "I will think of you every day," he said.

"And I will prepare bread for the time when we meet again," she answered.

They smiled an awkward smile at each other, then Jotham once again turned back toward the caravan. And, before he knew it, Jotham was on his way east, riding on the back of a donkey that was twice his age, and at the end of a line of camels that stretched as far as he could see. In the hours that followed, his heart was as full of peace as his belly was of Tabitha's bread. He just knew that within a day he'd be back with his family.

And that's when the caravan suddenly stopped and the leader rode back to where Jotham sat on his little donkey. The leader jumped off his camel and in one swift motion slapped Jotham hard across the face, knocking him to the ground. Jotham looked up in shock, his ears ringing and blood running from his mouth. The leader stood over him with a sneer on his face and the point of his sword sticking in Jotham's throat.

"Now, '*little one*'," he said, mocking Eliakim's name for Jotham. "We shall see what kind of *price* you bring!"

"Abraham was the father of Isaac," the Gospel of Matthew begins. "Isaac the father of Jacob, Jacob the father of Judah," and so on down through the generations, finally reaching "Joseph, the husband of Mary, of whom was born Jesus, who is called Christ."

Family heritage was important to the Jews of Jesus' day. It told who a man or woman was, who they were related to, how much they should be respected. So Matthew started his Gospel by showing other Jews that Jesus came from a long line of honored and respected men. It proved that Jesus was truly a Jew, and that he came from the line of David just as the prophets foretold.

Jotham is proud of his heritage, as are Eliakim and Tabitha. They always keep in mind where they have come from, and honor those who came before. As Christians, we too have a rich and honorable ancestry. We can each point to Jesus and say, "Like him, I am a child of the Most High

God." We can call Jesus our brother, and freely share with him in the riches of God's kingdom, even though there is an evil one who would like to sell us into slavery.

As we look forward to Christmas, and the celebration of Christ's birth, let us also look *back*, to the many generations of Christians and Jews who have passed on to us the Good News of Jesus. Let us thank God for the way he has worked to bring us knowledge of our Savior.

En Gedi Fool

Light the first violet candle.

Jotham lay on his back, a sharp stone digging into his ribs. He looked up at the face of the leader, and at the long, curved sword that threatened his neck. He gulped hard, and tried his best to hold very still.

The leader laughed, and the evil in it made Jotham tremble. The face that had seemed so kind a few hours ago was now a twisted mask of hate. His huge body towered over Jotham like a dragon from the tales told around campfires.

"Yes, we shall see what price we get for a worthless boy," he said again, laughing. Then turning to the men of his tribe he yelled, "Bind him!"

Rough and scratchy hands squeezed Jotham's arms and pulled him to his feet. Many others were gathered around now, and the women and children were laughing at him. The men stripped off his tunic and took his sandals, blanket, and food bag, leaving him with only his loin cloth to protect him from the cold. They pulled Jotham's arms roughly behind his back and tied his hands together so tightly it felt as if the rope would cut right through his wrists.

"Walk!" commanded one of the men, and pushed Jotham forward. Jotham stumbled, but caught himself before he fell. Sharp stones and needle-like thistles cut into his bare feet, but the pain in his heart was almost worse. Only moments ago he had been as happy as he always felt during the Feast of Trumpets, but now he felt as if he had been pushed off the edge of a deep, dark canyon.

"Move!" the man behind him roared, and he shoved Jotham once more. Jotham ran quickly to catch up with the end of the caravan, which was just starting to move again, and fell in line behind the last camel. Jotham's donkey was taken by a fat woman who sneered at him. The poor donkey bawled when the woman sat on him, but she beat him with a stick until he started to move.

The ground was cold under Jotham's feet, and covered with manure from the dozens of camels and stock that went ahead of him. He tried to step around the biggest piles, but the men that followed behind would whip him with a switch if he slowed down even a little. By the time the sun slid behind the hills, Jotham's feet were bleeding, and his back felt like a thousand bee stings from the switch.

Finally the caravan gathered in a field to the side of the road. Jotham was tied to an olive tree nearby. He watched as tents were quickly raised and fires built. His stomach groaned at the smell of baking bread and sizzling meat, but none was offered to him.

The rough bark of the tree cut into Jotham's skin, but it was the loneliness he felt that brought tears to his eyes. He had been so happy joining this caravan! He had thought he would find his family within a day. Now he was beginning to believe he would *never* see them again. If only I hadn't been so stubborn, he thought, I'd be with Mother and Father this very moment! He hung his head and cried bitterly, feeling just like he did the day his grandfather died.

Jotham watched as the caravan ate and drank and danced. He was so hungry he thought he could probably eat a whole camel all by himself. But then a boy just a little older than Jotham reached for a piece of sizzling meat that sat in front of the leader of the caravan. Moving as fast as a lion the leader drew his sword from his belt and cut off the boy's fingers just before they touched the meat. The boy grabbed his bleeding hand and fell back into the laps of some women. The leader put his face right up to the boy and said, "When I was twelve years old I killed my father and three of his wives because he would only feed me on Tuesdays and Thursdays! Don't ever try to take food from me again!"

There was a moment of shocked silence, then the leader sat back and all the people began eating and drinking and dancing again.

Suddenly the sting of the switch crossed Jotham's legs.

"Get up!" the man with the switch ordered. Not wanting to feel that sting again, Jotham stood to his feet as fast as he could slide up the tree trunk. The man untied Jotham's rope from the tree, then dragged him over to the largest of the tents. Maybe they're going to feed me! Jotham thought.

Instead, the man shoved Jotham over in front of the caravan's leader. Jotham began trembling as he eyed the blood on the leader's sword.

"Look at me!" the leader commanded. Jotham raised his head. "Open your mouth!" Jotham complied. The leader looked him over for a moment, then turned to the other man. "Take no less than three hundred sheckles," he said. "And don't try to cheat me!" Then he turned back to his eating and drinking.

Without a word, the man jerked the rope and pulled Jotham to his feet, then dragged him along behind. He mounted a donkey and started down the road, Jotham trailing on foot like a goat. Jotham's insides shivered in terror.

"Where … where are you taking me," Jotham asked.

The man kicked Jotham in the chest, knocking him to the ground. "Shut up, boy, or I'll roast you for my dinner!"

The rope went tight and Jotham was dragged through the rocks and thistles of the road until he scrambled to his feet. Now his knees and elbows were bleeding, and they stung like the worst of his father's spankings.

It seemed like hours later that they came over the top of a hill and saw a city below them. It had walls that were taller than the tops of trees, and it sat on the edge of a cliff overlooking a plain. In the bright moonlight Jotham saw a huge lake that began at the edge of the plain and went clear over the horizon. The Salt Sea, Jotham guessed. The sea of death.

The city itself was all lit up, with a lamp in almost every window and firelight glowing from inside the walls. Music drifted up from the city, and Jotham knew that he could very much enjoy this place, if it weren't for being tied up and led around like a camel.

Jotham felt a tug on the rope and began following the man down the road to the city gate. Guards stopped them there, guards that stood atop the walls and held long spears in their hands.

"Halt!" one of them yelled. "What business have you in En Gedi?"

"I come to sell some merchandise," the man yelled back. "A fine young boy who will make an excellent slave."

A slave, Jotham gasped to himself. He had half suspected this was the fate that awaited him, but hadn't let himself believe it. Suddenly he found himself yelling to the guard up in the tower.

"Please, sir! Help me! This man has … "

Jotham's head exploded with a slap from the back of his captor's hand. The guard only laughed.

"Very well then," he yelled down. "Enter the Dung Gate and take your business to the Court of Elders."

They moved forward again, passing huge piles of manure that smelled so bad Jotham held his breath. They entered the city through a creaky wooden door which opened in the larger gate. Once inside Jotham was amazed at all the sights and sounds. He had only been to cities on two other occasions, and was now overwhelmed as much by what he saw as by being a prisoner. Before he had time to wonder why women let scarlet scarves hang from their windows, or where the lively music was coming from, they had entered a large courtyard in the center of the city. Here people danced and sat drinking and argued about silly things. As they pushed through the crowd many eyes followed them. When they reached the center of the court, the man climbed on top of a wooden platform and pulled Jotham up next to him.

"I have for sale a small boy," he yelled over the crowd. "His name is … " He turned to Jotham and whispered. "What's yer name, boy?"

Jotham set his jaw and didn't answer, but then felt a stab of pain as the man twisted Jotham's arm behind his back. "Jotham," he said finally, hatred in his voice. "Jotham of Jericho."

The man turned back to the crowd. "His name's Jotham," he yelled. "A hard worker and a fine teller of tales. Who makes me an offer?"

"I'll give you twenty sheckles," a fat man with a bald head and red beard called out, laughing. The crowd laughed too, because they knew this was a small price.

"Do not insult your humble servant," the man roared, referring to himself. "For this humble servant serves Decha of Megiddo!"

Jotham had no idea who Decha of Megiddo was, but the crowd must have because they all stopped laughing. "Decha!" some of them gasped. "What's Decha doing around here?" another asked to no one in particular.

"For … forgive this fool," the fat man stuttered, "and honor me by accepting my bid of one hundred sheckles." A murmur rolled through the crowd and another man yelled, "I'll bid one hundred twenty!" And so it went for several minutes until the bid seemed to stop at three hundred eighty sheckles. Jotham watched all this in terror, trying to see each person who bid and what they might be like. He didn't like *any* of them, he decided, and was so scared he almost wet his loin cloth.

At that moment a new voice cut through the noise. "I bid seven hundred sheckles!" came the high-pitched squeal. The crowd gasped and turned to see who wanted this boy so badly. Jotham stretched his neck, trying to see who was about to become his new master. What he finally saw as the crowd parted was a skinny little man, his hands on his hips in defiance, dressed in rags and wearing a long, skinny hat that hung down to his waist. It was the hat, Jotham knew, of a fool, one who has been judged to be insane.

The crowd laughed at the fool, but with three cartwheels he landed at the foot of the platform and repeated his offer. "Seven hundred sheckles," he said again, blinking rapidly, "and not a sheckle more!"

Again the crowd laughed. "Away with you, fool," the servant of Decha ordered, "and let *sane* men conduct their business!" The fool shrieked and ran around in circles holding the edges of his hat. "*Sane* men! *Sane* men! Are you, sir, saying that the money of a fool is of no value?"

"Be gone I said! Or I shall take your head to decorate Decha's tent!"

"You'd take my head?" the fool screeched, grabbing his ears. "You'd take my *head!* If you take my head I shan't have a thought to give you," he said, running in circles again. Then he grabbed a bystander by the shoulders and shouted in his face, "He said he'd take my head! He said he'd take my head! How then would I see his awful face or speak the speech of men?" The bystander pushed the fool away. The servant of Decha drew his sword and dropped the rope that held Jotham.

"Yes, I shall take your head," he roared. "I shall take it and I shall feed it to the rats!"

At that the fool shrieked once more, then ran over to the platform and threw himself across it at the feet of the servant, his arms spread wide. "Then be quick about it," he shouted, "for I must get home to fly my kite!"

Decha's servant let out a roar that burst with anger. His eyes wide and his face snarled in a look of red hatred, he raised the broad sword high over his head and aimed for the fool's neck. But just as he brought the sword down with a "swoosh," the fool jumped up, grabbed Jotham's rope and gave it a mighty yank. Jotham flew forward, off the platform, and into the arms of the fool, just as the sword sliced into the wooden platform. But since his target was no longer there, the servant lost his balance and flew head first off the platform and into the dirt, screaming.

The fool, with Jotham in his arms, ducked under the platform and came out the other side. He pushed through the crowd, who cheered as if this were a festival performance, then ran down a dark, narrow side street. Behind them Jotham could hear Decha's servant screaming his threats, but the fool just kept running. As they approached the Dung Gate, the fool began yelling, "Leper! Leper!" and the guards quickly opened the door and jumped back.

Once outside, the fool set Jotham on his feet and, pulling him by the rope, yelled, "Run like the wind, child, or we shall both be headless by morning!" They crossed a field of grain, then climbed quickly into the hills. They passed some pools of water that shimmered in the moonlight, then ran through a shallow creek. The fool led Jotham through winding trails and up steep cliffs before finally pulling him inside a small cave.

Both of them were gasping great breaths of air, and Jotham felt the dust of the cave stick to his sweaty skin. The fool swept the hat off his head, then quickly untied Jotham's hands. "Worry not, child," he said, breathing hard but sounding quite sane now. "I know these caves as no other does. I could hide you here for centuries before anyone found you."

And Jotham trembled, wondering if this fool could really be his savior.

Isaiah clearly told the people of Israel how the Messiah would appear. "Therefore the Lord himself will give you a sign," he said. "The virgin will be with child and will give birth to a son, and will call him Immanuel" (Is 7:14).

But still, the Jews expected their Messiah to come as a powerful King with a mighty army, a King who would destroy the Romans and give them back their land. They forgot what the prophecy had told them, and instead believed what their anger and hatred *wanted* them to believe.

God's ways are not man's ways, and just as Jotham was saved by someone who was thought to be a fool, so our own salvation came in a very unexpected way. It came in the form of a tiny baby born to a poor carpenter and his wife.

Jotham still must search for his family, just as we must sometimes still search to understand what God desires of us. But if we believe in the one who saved us from our enemy, and make for him a sacrifice of our lives, he promises a rich and abundant life, both on earth and in heaven.

Salt Sea

Light the first violet candle.

Voices drifted up from the valley. Men's voices. Angry voices.

"The servant of Decha has hired men to search for us," the fool whispered. Even in the dark of the cave, Jotham could see he had a little smile on his face. "No matter," he continued. "They will not find us. And soon they will give up. Hired men have little desire to spend a cold night searching for another man's enemy."

Jotham looked at the fool in the little light that found its way into the cave. He looked quite normal, Jotham decided. Not at all like a fool. About the same age as his father, but with short hair and no beard. As soon as they entered the cave, the fool had pulled some dead bushes across the opening to hide it. It was a dark night, and Jotham figured that no one could possibly see the entrance to the cave.

"Why do you wear the hat of a fool?" he asked finally.

The man smiled. "I have found it beneficial at times to appear as someone harmless."

Jotham thought about that for a moment, then nodded. "I guess it worked tonight," he said.

"Yes, it did, though I wasn't sure for a moment," the fool said, rubbing his neck.

Jotham knew he should thank the fool, but found it difficult to get the words out. "Sir Fool, I want to … I mean it was … "

"There's no need," the fool said, raising his hand. "You are most welcome. I often find myself the rescuer of small boys in peril." Then he added, "And you may call me Nathan of the Essenes."

"I am Jotham of Jericho."

"Shalom, Jotham. And how did you come to be in such a nasty place as En Gedi?"

"I … I was chasing a lion away from my flock," Jotham started, but then went silent. He hung his head and started again, quietly. "I got mad at my father and ran away. He thought I was killed by a jackal, and moved on without me."

Nathan thought about this for a moment. "It is a dangerous path your anger has chosen. I will help you all that I can, but now it is time to rest, Jotham of Jericho. We must leave this place as soon as it is safe."

Nathan pulled a large tunic from a bag hidden in the cave and gave it to Jotham, then filled him with cheese and water from the same bag. "Who is Decha?" Jotham asked.

"An evil man, full of hate and vengeance. He comes from the North, a place called Meggido."

"Why is he here?"

"No one knows for certain," Nathan answered, "but I heard he is searching for something. Or someone."

Jotham finished the last bite of cheese and then was asleep, feeling once again that he was in the company of a friend.

But the bared teeth of the jackal dripped with Jotham's blood once more, and he bolted awake with a cry.

"Child, what is it," Nathan asked, startled awake by the scream.

"A jackal," Jotham panted, "a jackal in my dreams. He knows … "

Nathan prodded when Jotham didn't continue. "Knows what, boy?"

"He knows I'm … afraid of jackals."

Nathan smiled. "It is no dishonor to fear a wild beast, Jotham." Then he sighed and stood up. "Jackals are dangerous animals. Especially the *two*-legged kind. It is best to travel while our enemies sleep," he whispered.

Quietly they gathered their things and left the cave, walking north, away from En Gedi. As they picked their way through the deep ravines and jagged rocks, Jotham worried that he was leaving his family behind.

"I do not believe it is so," Nathan told him when Jotham mentioned this. "I have been in En Gedi for four days and no caravan has entered or passed. Such things do not go unnoticed."

Jotham spent so much time wondering about his family that, before he knew it, the sun was straight overhead and they had walked away the morning. Just after sunrise they had met the shores of the salt sea, and had followed it north ever since.

"What's a kite?" Jotham asked finally, the sting of salt filling every breath.

"A what?" Nathan answered.

"A kite. You told that bad man that you had to get home to fly your kite."

Nathan laughed deep and loud. "Oh that. Well, a kite is a magical toy that flies through the air. I saw it myself when I traveled to Persia many years ago. They fly as quick as a bird, and as high as the stars … "

Nathan was lost in thought now, staring into the sky. "'Therefore a star shall come from Jacob,'" he said finally, "'a scepter shall rise out of Israel.' Do you know what that means, Jotham?"

Jotham thought for a moment. "That the spirit of our father Jacob is in the stars?"

Nathan laughed, but it was a kind laugh. "No, child, though that is a good thought. But in truth it means that the Messiah shall come to us from the family of Jacob. It is one way in which we will *know* he is the Messiah."

"What other way is there," Jotham asked.

Nathan thought for a moment, then recited, "'But you, oh Bethlehem, though you are small among the clans of Judah, out of you will come for me one who will be ruler over Israel, whose origins are from of old, from ancient times.'"

Jotham frowned a thoughtful frown. "Does that mean the Messiah will be born in Bethlehem?"

"Yes indeed. It is how Jehovah has ordained it to be."

"Give me another," Jotham said eagerly.

"'Know and understand this,'" Nathan quoted. "'From the issuing of the decree to restore and rebuild Jerusalem until the Anointed One, the ruler, comes, there will be seven "sevens" and sixty-two sevens.'"

This one made no sense at all to Jotham. "What does that mean?" he asked.

Nathan sighed a deep sigh and said, "It means, my young friend, that I am in disfavor with my elders." Jotham didn't understand this at all, and the look on his face said so. Nathan laughed. "Forgive my little joke," he said. "I believe it means," and here he became suddenly very serious, "I believe it means that we are very near the time of the Messiah."

Jotham's eyes grew as wide as the sun. "How near?" he whispered.

Nathan stopped and knelt down next to Jotham, looking him in the eye. "I believe, Jotham of Jericho, it means the Messiah could arrive any day."

Jotham had never heard such talk before. There had been stories of the Messiah for as long as he could remember, but always they were far off in the future, many generations from now. The thought that the Messiah could come during Jotham's lifetime was … well … laughable!

Jotham laughed a big laugh. "You're joking with me again," he said. But Nathan's face remained dead serious, and soon Jotham stopped laughing. "But how do you know that?" he asked, suspicious.

Nathan smiled. "It is all in the Scriptures," he said, "for anyone who chooses to read them."

They started walking again, and Jotham thought long and hard about these things. Then his stomach began to growl. He was about to mention that lunch might be a good idea when they rounded a bend and a village came into sight.

"Where are we?" Jotham gasped.

"This is Qumran, my home."

As they approached the village, Jotham could see men in long robes walking about, and many young boys carrying water bags or clay jars or long bundles wrapped in cloth. But of all the people he saw, Jotham saw no women. "Where are all the women?" Jotham asked, trailing Nathan by two paces. "And why are there so many boys here?"

"We have no women in Qumran," Nathan answered, his back to Jotham. "And we bring the boys here from wherever we can find them."

And with those words, a cold chill ran up Jotham's spine.

God provided the people of Israel with many hints about how, where, and when Jesus would be born. He gave them all the information they needed to recognize the Messiah so that they could believe in and follow him.

God has provided *us* with many hints and instructions as well. He has given us all the information *we* need to know how to live holy and unselfish lives. But do we? Do we search the Scriptures daily until we know them by heart? And then do we do what God has commanded, following the example of Jesus, so that we love others more than ourselves?

Advent is the perfect time to begin a habit of spending time with God each day. It's the perfect time to develop a habit of reading his Word daily, even if it's just a verse or two. And it's the perfect time to begin the habit of acting unselfishly toward others.

Jotham is learning the importance of studying the Scriptures and then living the way God tells us is best. Are you ready to do the same?

Qumran

Light the first violet candle.

Jotham stopped dead in his tracks, the icy fingers of fear wrapped around his heart. Nathan had seemed so nice—maybe *too* nice. Was all this just a ploy to kidnap Jotham and make him a child-slave of Qumran?

Nathan kept walking, and Jotham felt like he should turn and run. But to where? He was in the middle of the Wilderness of Judea, next to a sea of death, with no idea where to go. Yet panic gripped his legs and he could not make himself walk into a village where children were slaves. So he stood there on the verge of tears, his fear pulling him in seven different directions.

Finally Nathan noticed that Jotham was no longer behind him. Turning back he walked toward Jotham and Jotham walked backwards, away from Nathan, trying to decide if he should run.

"Jotham! What is it? What has frightened you so?"

Jotham's eyes were locked on the face that had seemed so kind. He had seen kind faces before, and knew you couldn't always tell what was be*hind* such a face.

"Did you see a snake," Nathan asked, "or step on a scorpion?" Jotham slowly shook his head "no" and continued to stare. He'd seen many snakes this day, and even a few scorpions. He wondered again if he was staring at one of them right now.

Suddenly Nathan understood. "It's the children, isn't it?" he said. "You think I'm kidnapping you, correct?" Jotham nodded his head, and compassion swept across Nathan's face. He knelt down next to Jotham and put his hand on the boy's shoulder. "Jotham, trust me, I am not bringing you to harm. These children are here because they *want* to be. We take in orphans from all over the land, training them in the ways of the Lord. We provide a safe and comfortable home for them, but they are free to leave anytime they wish. Just as you are."

It's true, Jotham now realized, that there were no walls around the village, and only one guard in a tower. Nothing to keep the children there if they wished to leave. Then he watched as three boys ran out from the gate. They were laughing as they jumped into the water to swim. Finally, the trembling in Jotham's stomach began to calm and he started breathing again.

Nathan smiled. "Come now, let us go meet some new friends."

Jotham was still a little hesitant, but relaxed more as they came near Qumran. As they entered the town, Jotham now saw that all the children were happy. As he had first seen, many were hard at work, but many more were playing or talking. The men in robes, though, all had sour faces, and they seemed to take everything very seriously.

"Why are all the men so angry?" Jotham asked.

"They are not angry, Jotham. They are deep in thought." Then seeing that this puzzled the boy, he explained. "We Essenes have devoted our lives to studying the Scriptures. We spend our days reading and copying and thinking about the words of Jehovah. Most of us do not marry, and very few of us ever leave Qumran. It is our service to the Holy One."

Jotham next saw that some of the boys were working in pairs, carrying buckets of rocks suspended on poles. They lifted the buckets to men working high on wooden platforms. "What are those men doing?" he asked.

"Rebuilding the walls of Qumran," Nathan answered. "Less than two years ago all you see here now was nothing but rubble." Jotham shot Nathan a questioning look and Nathan simply replied, "Romans." As he spoke, Nathan seemed almost to be in pain. "They destroyed Qumran many years ago. But last year, many of us decided to rebuild, as you see. We have all vowed that we shall defend Qumran forever, even if it means our own deaths."

Jotham was silent as they walked, then finally asked, "What's in there?" pointing to a row of rectangular buildings with high roofs.

"Those are the scribes' rooms where we copy the Scriptures. Come, I'll show you."

Nathan led Jotham through a wooden door that creaked loudly when it was opened. Inside were rows of tables. Each table had an oil lamp on it, and at each sat a man in a long robe, hunched over a piece of parchment paper. "We take the Holy Scriptures," Nathan whispered, "and copy the words from one parchment to another, so that many people may hear the words of Jehovah. That man there," he continued, pointing to a tall skinny man with no hair who stood at the front of the room, "reads each letter from the original parchment, and then all these other men write that letter onto their copies."

Jotham listened as the man at the front called out, "Cheth!" He knew that this was a letter of the alphabet, and watched as all the men at the tables dipped their quills in ink and carefully began drawing that letter onto their parchments. When all had finished, the man at the front called out "Cheth" again, and every man looked to make sure he had written down the correct letter. Satisfied that the letter had been properly written onto each parchment, the tall, skinny man called out "Samekh," the next letter in whatever word he was spelling. Jotham had never seen anything like this. "Do they do this all day?" he asked finally.

"All day and every day, except the Sabbath," Nathan answered. "In this way we will have twenty new copies of the Torah in less than two years."

"Twenty copies," Jotham gasped in amazement.

"Yes indeed," Nathan answered. "It is truly a modern-day miracle!"

After watching four letters being copied—a process that took most of an hour—they left the scribe building and headed toward some buildings that looked like houses. Just then a taller man approached. He wore the same kind of long robe, but was much fatter than the other men. A skinny, vulture-like man followed a pace behind. "Nathan! I will speak with you," the first man called out.

Nathan groaned under his breath, but aloud said, "Yes, Rabbi, what is it?"

Jotham knew that "rabbi" meant "teacher," even though he'd never had one himself. He figured that this must be the man in charge of the other Essenes.

"You know *exactly* what it is!" the Rabbi said as he walked up. "You have once again been spreading your tales of the Messiah against my specific orders!" Then the Rabbi saw Jotham for the first time and added, "I'd wager you've even told this young boy here!"

Nathan sighed deeply. "Rabbi," he said evenly, "I spread no tales except those which are clearly told in Scripture."

The Rabbi's face turned purple, and Jotham thought his head might pop like a grape. "Now see here, Nathan! I was studying the Scriptures before your parents ever laid eyes on each other, and I know perfectly well they say nothing of the tales you spread! The Messiah *will* come to us, but we must tarry for many generations before we are worthy of his arrival!"

Now Nathan began to turn red, and Jotham could see this was an old argument. "We don't *need* to be worthy," he said, his voice beginning to rise. "We can *never* be worthy! The whole purpose of the Messiah is to cleanse us in our unworthiness!"

The argument went back and forth for several minutes, and Jotham wondered if he ever *would* get lunch. Nathan kept trying to point out what the Scriptures said about the Messiah coming, and the Rabbi kept arguing that they had to become perfect before the Messiah would appear. All the while the skinny, vulture-like man, whom Jotham figured out was the Rabbi's assistant, stood back smiling, obviously pleased at Nathan's predicament.

"Nathan," the Rabbi said finally, "I am in charge here and you *will* do as I say or face discipline from the Council of Elders!"

"Discipline!" Nathan exploded. "Discipline! For reading the Scriptures and seeing in them the truth?"

The Rabbi started to answer but was interrupted by a shout from the guard tower.

"Riders! Five men on horses riding fast from the south!"

Nathan's eyes widened and he looked at the Rabbi, the argument of a moment ago forgotten. "Decha of Megiddo," he gasped. "I saved this boy from his clutches in En Gedi and now he comes for him. I did not believe he would care enough to look this far."

The Rabbi's face melted into concern and compassion. Looking at Jotham he said, "You must take the boy and hide quickly!" They ran toward the back of the village where the hills behind came almost straight down. "Here," the Rabbi said, stopping at a cook tent, "take food and water and go hide in the library."

Jotham watched as they quickly filled the bags, and wondered what a "library" was. Then they were running again, into the foothills. Bits of rock and dirt flew into Jotham's face as he followed Nathan up the steep cliffs. Far below and out toward the edge of the salt sea were the riders, and Jotham could tell from the long colorful coat that the one in the lead was indeed Decha of Megiddo.

Soon they climbed over the top of a ridge and Jotham saw that a thousand caves dotted the hills. They climbed so fast and so hard and so far that Jotham thought his legs would surely collapse, but soon Nathan pulled him into a small cave. When Jotham's eyes adjusted to the darkness they grew wide in amazement. At the back of the cave, stretching as far as he could see, were rows of tall, narrow clay pots.

"What are *those?*" Jotham gasped.

Nathan looked to see what Jotham had spotted, then smiled. "Those are our manuscripts," he said. "They are the original documents from which we copy all the Holy Scriptures."

Jotham gently touched the rough side of the closest urn. "May I see one?" he asked in hushed reverence. He had never until today even seen a *copy* of the Holy Scriptures, and now here he was in a cave that held the *real* ones.

"Later, perhaps," Nathan said. "When the danger has passed."

They sat on the dirt floor of the cave with their backs against the stone wall. "And so we spend another night in a cave together," Nathan said, smiling. Jotham smiled back. He felt safe here in this cave with Nathan, and thought how wonderful it was to have such a friend.

But then both of their smiles vanished as the sound of falling rocks shot through the cave.

Jesus said to the men on the road to Emmaus, "How foolish you are, and how slow of heart to believe all that the Prophets have spoken!… And beginning with Moses and all the Prophets, he explained to them what was said in all the Scriptures concerning himself" (Lk 24:25-27).

Sometimes people don't understand what the Bible really says because they don't read it for themselves. Sometimes they don't understand because they were taught a certain thing and think that to change their minds or learn something new would make them look like a fool. And sometimes they don't understand just because they don't believe that God can really do what he said he'll do.

Nathan has read the Scriptures and understands what they say. But his teacher refuses to believe that the Messiah will really come as the prophets said, because it would change everything he's ever been taught.

Maybe this Christmas season would be a good time to check your beliefs about who Jesus was and is against the truths found in Scripture. You may find that some of the things you say and do in his name are not really like him at all. And you'll certainly find that the man we call Christ is waiting for you with open and unselfish arms, whether you are perfect or not.

Urns and Scrolls

Light the first two violet candles.

Nathan sat perfectly still, his eyes and ears searching the air for a hint of who was outside the cave. Jotham's heart jumped as the clatter of falling rocks pierced the silence once more. Nathan stood carefully so as not to make a sound, and crept silently over to the mouth of the cave. Staying in the shadows he peeked outside. Once again broken bits of rock fell, and this time Nathan saw that they fell right in front of the cave entrance. Decha's men were surrounding the cave, he realized.

Nathan motioned for Jotham to come to him, then whispered in his ear. "I will distract them," he said. "Run down the hill as fast as you can, but do not go back to Qumran. Go to Jericho, a half-day's walk to the north. Find there a merchant named Silas. He is a friend."

Jotham's eyes grew wide and he rapidly shook his head "no." But Nathan gave him a stern look and wagged his finger at him as if to say, "Mind me!"

Jotham hung his head and nodded slightly. He didn't want to leave Nathan, who would surely be killed. The thought of Nathan dying just to save Jotham made Jotham's heart ache like it never had before. All this is happening because I wouldn't mind Father, he thought, and tears started running down his face.

Nathan put on his fool's hat, then held up three fingers and counted with them. "Three … two … one … " As his last finger dropped, Nathan ran screaming out of the cave. Jotham followed a step behind, crying. He ran right past Nathan, who had stopped and turned toward their attackers. He wasn't exactly sure which way to go, but started climbing down as fast as he could. His heart was racing and he knocked his knee hard on a rock. Behind him he heard Nathan screaming, and the sound made Jotham shake uncontrollably.

"Jotham, come back!" he heard behind him. It was Decha's men, and he wasn't *about* to listen to them. "Jotham, come!" the voice called again. "It's all right!" This time the voice had a funny sound to it, Jotham thought. It sounds almost like … like … Nathan!

Jotham stopped and turned, looking back up the hill. There he saw Nathan, standing in front of the cave, hands on his hips, and he was laughing.

Laughing!? For a moment Jotham didn't understand, but then he saw a flock of goats grazing on some tufts of grass above the cave, and suddenly he understood.

And then *he* began to laugh, too.

Jotham felt the fear of a moment ago flow down from his head and out through his toes. They both stood there laughing at themselves for being scared by some goats, but mostly they were just relieved. Jotham decided then and there to be nice to every goat he ever met from then on!

Nathan stopped laughing and motioned Jotham to come quickly. Jotham followed his friend's gaze and then he, too, saw the men climbing into the hills far below. He scrambled back up the rocks and into the cave, with Nathan right behind him.

"They will not find us," Nathan assured Jotham. "There are thousands of caves up here, and this is the least obvious of all. That is why we chose it for our library."

Jotham wasn't so sure about their safety. He figured if goats could find them, so could Decha's men. But he moved to the back of the cave and sat again among the urns that held the Holy Scriptures. "What's a 'library?'" Jotham asked after a while.

"It is a place where writings are collected and stored, such as the Holy Scriptures behind you."

Jotham looked again at the clay urns, then asked, "Will you read some to me?"

Nathan looked toward the mouth of the cave, trying to decide if it was safe to read aloud. "All right," he said finally. "But you must sit close so I can read softly." Jotham watched as Nathan made a torch from a stick of wood and a strip of cloth, lighting it with a flint stone against the wall of the cave. Then, slowly, he eased the top off one of the urns and pulled out a roll of yellow parchment wrapped in sheepskin. He bowed slightly and said a short prayer which Jotham didn't understand, then carefully unrolled the parchment and began to read.

Nathan read stories such as Jotham had never heard before. Jotham knew the *big* stories, of course, like Noah and Moses. But Nathan was reading him stories of men like Samson, Gideon, and David.

"So David triumphed over the Philistine with a sling and a stone," Nathan read, "without a sword in his hand he struck down the Philistine and killed him."

"How can that be!" Jotham exclaimed. "A young boy against such a giant!"

Nathan patted Jotham on the shoulder. "Fear is a powerful weapon you give to your enemy, Jotham," Nathan said. "Whether that enemy is a Philistine … or a jackal. David gave his fear to Jehovah, and in turn Jehovah made David a strong and powerful man."

Jotham nodded his head, then Nathan kept reading.

"'He was despised and rejected by men,'" he read. "'A man of sorrows, and familiar with suffering … Surely he took up our weaknesses, and carried our sorrows, yet we considered him stricken by God, smitten by him, and afflicted. But he was pierced for our transgressions, he was crushed for our sins; the punishment that brought us peace was upon him, and by his wounds we are healed.'"

Jotham looked puzzled. "Who is that talking about?" he asked.

"These are the words of Jehovah as spoken by the Holy Prophet Isaiah," Nathan answered, "and they speak of the Messiah."

Jotham's eyes grew wide. "But I thought the Messiah was coming to kill the Romans."

Nathan nodded. "Yes, that is what many think. But Isaiah clearly tells us that it is the *Messiah* who is to suffer and die. He will suffer and die to pay for our sins, just like the lambs we sacrifice for our sin offering."

This was all quite new and puzzling to Jotham. "What about that Bethlehem story you told yesterday?"

Nathan drew another scroll from the urn, then said, "These are the words of Jehovah as spoken by the Holy Prophet Micah. 'But you, oh Bethlehem, though you are small among the clans of Judah, out of you will come for me one who will be ruler over Israel, whose origins are from of old, from ancient times.'"

"Does that mean that Bethlehem is very old?"

"No no," Nathan said. "It means that the one who *comes* from Bethlehem, the *Messiah,* is 'from of old, from ancient times.' It means the Messiah has existed since the beginning of all things."

"So he's an old man in Bethlehem?"

Nathan chuckled. "No, Jotham. The Messiah shall come as the Holy Prophet Isaiah told us, 'Unto you a child is born, to us a son is given.'"

"But *whose* son?" Jotham asked, exasperated. "And how can one who is old be a baby?"

Nathan carefully set the scroll down, then looked Jotham in the eye. "The Messiah is 'from of old' but will still be born as a baby because the Messiah, Jotham, is the Son of God."

Jotham's eyes grew wide. He had never heard such a thing! The Messiah, the Son of God? It seemed ridiculous.

"Did you check that one?" The voice coming in from outside the cave shocked them both and they instantly fell quiet. It had come from some distance away, but still close enough they could easily hear the men talking.

"I'll check it, then," the voice said, and Jotham began to tremble again.

"Be calm, little one," Nathan whispered as he smothered the torch in the dirt. "They are still far off," and he hugged Jotham close. They sat there together silently for a long time, and finally the light began to fade. Occasionally they heard the men talking, but it was always far away. As he sat there, Jotham thought of the things that Nathan had said, and he began to understand how the Messiah really could come as a baby instead of as a king, like he'd always been taught.

As the cave grew dark, Jotham's eyes became heavy, and soon he was asleep. The next thing he knew the cave was light again, and Nathan was shaking him awake.

"Jotham, wake up," Nathan hissed. "Decha's men are right outside!"

"But you, Bethlehem … though you are small … out of you will come for me one who will be ruler over Israel, whose origins are from of old" (Mi 5:2).

Today we light the second candle, the Bethlehem candle. It is to remind us that Christ was born as a human baby, so that God might fully understand the pains, heartaches, joys, and sorrows we go through as humans.

And that's why the Bethlehem candle could also be called the *Hope* candle. Our hope lies in the fact that God loves us enough that he came to us in the form of a baby, to live among us, to allow us to see him.

Jotham still doesn't fully understand about the Messiah. He had always been taught that the Messiah would be a powerful king who would destroy the Romans. He doesn't yet understand that the Messiah was coming to teach love, not hate. But if he did understand, if he knew what we know today, he could look toward Bethlehem with us and say those words from Isaiah, "but those who hope in the Lord will renew their strength. They will soar on wings like eagles; they will run and not grow weary, they will walk and not be faint" (Is 40:31).

Jotham's Line

Light the first two violet candles.

Nathan motioned for Jotham to hold very still. He was crouched by the entrance to the cave, a large rock in hand. Jotham could hear voices outside, and they were much nearer than they had been the day before.

"I'd kill Decha myself," a voice said right outside the cave, "if I thought I could get a shekel for his bones!" The other voices mocked the speaker, and called him a liar.

Finally the voices drifted off and for a long time Jotham heard no sound except his own breathing, which he did as little as possible. He drank the last of the water, and was working on the last of the cheese, when footsteps were heard approaching. They came straight toward the mouth of the cave and Nathan raised his rock, ready to strike.

"Would the library mice care to see the daylight?" It was the Rabbi, Jotham saw. He had stuck his fat, bald head through the doorway, and Nathan had almost splattered him before he recognized the Rabbi's red beard.

"Welcome, Rabbi," Nathan said breathlessly, "and yes, we would very much like to see the daylight again. Come, Jotham!"

On the way down the hill, the Rabbi explained that Decha and his men had left two hours before, convinced that the "fool" and the boy were nowhere near. Decha had commanded the Rabbi to report any sighting of the two, and the Rabbi had assured him he would. "May Jehovah forgive my lies," he said, shaking his head.

"I'm sure he will," Nathan answered.

The Rabbi's assistant walked with them as well, and now he nudged the Rabbi, as if pushing him someplace he didn't want to go. Nervously, the Rabbi spoke.

"Uh, Nathan, this idea of yours for keeping orphaned boys at Qumran … it doesn't, uh, seem to be working out very well … "

Nathan gave the Rabbi's assistant a scowl, then said to the Rabbi, "There is only one among us who feels that way, Rabbi."

"Yes, well, still it has always been our rule that there be no women or children at Qumran and I believe that is best."

"Best for who? Certainly not for the boys!"

"Now, Nathan, you know that we established Qumran as a place where we can perfect ourselves for Jehovah. It's a place of study, not a place where we … we … "

"Care for Jehovah's lost children?" Nathan finished the sentence for the Rabbi.

"Oh Nathan! Don't be so dramatic. I'm sure Jehovah understands that we don't have the time or resources to … to … "

"To love other people in his name?" Nathan finished once again.

"Now that is enough, Nathan!"

But Nathan was angry. "'Woe to the shepherds of Israel who only take care of themselves!'" he quoted from Scripture.

The Rabbi turned bright red. "You … I … Oh never mind," he said finally, stomping off. Nathan grinned at the Rabbi's assistant, who only scowled and followed after the Rabbi.

Back in Qumran now, Nathan led Jotham to a long, low building. Here, Nathan explained, was where all the boys lived. They soon found Jotham some clothes that fit better than the tent Nathan's tunic had been. Finally they had a meal of veal steaks and bread. Afterward, Nathan took Jotham for a walk down to the Salt Sea.

"Jotham, I would like to speak to you about the future," Nathan said as they walked.

"You mean about the coming of the Messiah?" Jotham asked, taking practice shots with his sling as they talked.

Nathan laughed. "No, no, I mean your very near future, such as *tomorrow.*" Nathan turned serious again, and continued. "You must know that you are welcome to stay here with us as long as you would like. You will be given a job like the other boys, of course, but we will care for you and feed and clothe you like the other boys as well. And," he added with a smile, "we will teach you the ways of Jehovah."

Jotham thought about this for a long time as they walked. He had been gone from his family for more than a week now, and the way his family travelled, they might be anywhere in Palestine by now. But still, he couldn't bear the thought of leaving them forever.

"I thank you for your offer, Nathan, but I must continue to search for my family. They must be somewhere near here, and I will never find them if I don't look because they don't know to look for me. Nor would they look in Qumran." Jotham hated having people tell him what to do, but he was beginning to understand that sometimes he had to submit to those older than he, so he added, "With your permission, I will leave Qumran tomorrow to find my father."

Nathan frowned. "I understand your feelings, Jotham, but I cannot allow one so young to wander alone through the wilderness of Judea. Nor can I leave my duties here in Qumran to accompany you." Jotham's hope vanished in an instant and his heart began to ache once more. "Therefore," Nathan continued, "I will take you tomorrow to Jericho, to my friend Silas. He will help you find a safe caravan with which to travel."

Jotham's heart now burst with joy and he jumped up and down excitedly. "Oh thank you, Nathan, thank you! I will give you half of my father's sheep when I find him!"

Nathan laughed. "I think you should probably discuss that with your father. But you are welcome just the same."

By now they had reached the edge of the Salt Sea. Jotham's nose stung with the salty smell, but it was not an unpleasant odor. Several of the boys from Qumran were swimming, and yelled at Jotham to join them. Jotham gave Nathan a questioning look, and Nathan smiled and nodded his head, so Jotham stripped off his clothes and ran into the water.

"I will see you at the evening meal," Nathan called after him, and then turned back to Qumran.

Jotham shuddered as the cold water closed around him. He swam out to the other boys and introduced himself. One of the other boys said, "I am Otham of Galilee." "I am Boaz of Ramah," said another. They all introduced themselves, but it was the last one that Jotham remembered. "I am Bartholomew of Talmai," he said, and Jotham thought he looked like the kind of person who could be a good friend.

The boys splashed and played together, and Jotham thought how strange the water felt. It was smooth and slippery, almost slimy. And when he went into the water deeper than his waist he couldn't touch the bottom or stand up no matter how hard he tried. It was as if the water were a living creature, pushing him up off the bottom. When he swam or floated, almost his entire body would be out of the water, just as if he were lying on a board.

Jotham thought this all very strange and magical, but Bartholomew explained it was because of the salt in the water. "There is so much salt," he said, "that the grains stack up one on top of the other and hold you up." Jotham stared into the water for a long time trying to see the grains but he couldn't, and he wondered if Bartholomew really knew what he was talking about.

When the boys were done swimming they rinsed off in a nearby creek, then headed for one of the long buildings. "It is time for the evening meal," Bartholomew explained.

Inside were several long rows of heavy wooden tables. All the men sat at the far end of the room, and all the boys at the near end. Jotham sat next to Bartholomew. The Rabbi thanked Jehovah for the food, then three men began serving bowls of stew. They had just started eating, and Jotham was just about to ask Bartholomew why everyone was so quiet, when Nathan stood up at the far end of the table, holding a scroll.

"It is written in the first book of the Torah by our Holy Father, Moses," he said, "'The scepter will not depart from Judah, nor the ruler's staff from between his feet, until he comes to whom it belongs, and the obedience of the nations is his.'"

All the men and boys said, "Selah!" then Nathan continued. "These are the words our Holy Father, Jacob, spoke to his son, Judah. It is clear that Jehovah is telling us that the Messiah shall come from the line of Judah … "

"What line are *you* from," Bartholomew whispered to Jotham.

"Huh?"

"I said what *line* are you from?"

Jotham shrugged his shoulders. "I don't think I'm from *any* line."

At this Bartholomew let out a loud laugh. "You have to be from *some* line," he said.

At Bartholomew's laugh Nathan stopped talking and everyone else stopped eating. They all turned and looked at the two boys. Jotham felt himself blush and wanted to climb under the table. "Uh … for … forgive me, Nathan," Bartholomew stuttered. "I was just … uh … trying to make our new friend feel welcome … "

Nathan gave them both a stern look and the Rabbi said he would see Bartholomew in private after the meal. Then Nathan continued.

"So we see through the Holy Scriptures, that the Messiah shall descend from the line of Judah."

Everyone said, "Selah," again, and the Rabbi added, "But not in our lifetime, eh, Nathan?"

Nathan smiled. "I shall concede, Rabbi, that this particular passage does not tell us *when* the Messiah shall reveal himself."

Everyone laughed at this, relieved that Nathan had avoided yet another argument about the coming of the Messiah.

After the meal Jotham caught up with Nathan outside the dining hall. "Where shall I sleep this night?" he asked.

"Well, you may go back up to the cave if you wish," Nathan said with a smile, "or you may sleep in the dormitory with Bartholomew."

Jotham grinned. "I would like that very much." Then he turned serious again and asked, "Nathan, what line am I from?"

Nathan frowned and stroked his chin. "Well, let me see. You said your father is from … " Nathan thought for a moment, making gestures in the air with his finger, then finally said, "I believe, Jotham, if I know your father's lineage correctly, that you would be of the line of Judah."

Jotham's eyes grew big. "The same as the Messiah!" he gasped.

"Yes, indeed."

"Thank you, Nathan," he whispered, barely able to get the words out. He walked to the dormitory just as Bartholomew arrived. He could see that Bartholomew had been crying. He was rubbing his bottom.

"The Rabbi wanted to make sure I remembered not to talk during teachings," he said, pouting.

Bartholomew helped Jotham fix a bed next to his, and soon it was dark and all the boys were asleep. All, that is, except Jotham. He lay there, staring out the window at the strange star he'd been watching since his first night with Eliakim. "Mother," he whispered to the star, "I am related to the Messiah!"

The Bible tells us, "Both the one who makes men holy and those who are made holy are of the same family. So Jesus is not ashamed to call them brothers" (Heb 2:11).

This means that we who hold Christ as our Savior have become brothers or sisters to Jesus. We are now of the same family, just as if we all had the same last name.

Jotham is amazed that he might be related to the Messiah. Perhaps *we* should also be amazed—amazed that our perfect and holy God has chosen to adopt us into his family.

So as you wait for Christmas Day, remember that what you're waiting for is the birthday of your Brother!

Jericho

Light the first two violet candles.

Something was kicking Jotham in the behind and he didn't much like it. He was still sound asleep and had every intention of staying that way.

"Jotham, get up!" It was the second time Jotham had heard the voice, and this time he recognized it as that of Bartholomew.

"It's time for morning prayers," Bartholomew whispered, as other boys looked at him crossly for talking.

Jotham opened one eye just enough to see, then mumbled, "I don't feel like praying today." He had been awake very late thinking about what Nathan had said last night and had only slept a few hours.

"You *must* go to morning prayers," Bartholomew pleaded. "*Everyone* must go."

But Jotham ignored Bartholomew. After a moment a sly look crossed Bartholomew's face, and he said in a taunting voice, "The Rabbi will be most displeased if you're not at morning prayers … "

Jotham's eyes shot open as he remembered the "lesson" the Rabbi had taught Bartholomew the night before. In moments he was out of bed and dressed, not wanting his bottom to suffer the same fate.

The prayers were said in a small synagogue by a garden, then the morning meal was served. Bartholomew didn't utter a word during the teachings. Afterward Jotham helped him do his chores, which involved moving the big clay urns from the pottery building where they had been baked, to the room where the Scriptures were copied.

The sun had moved an hour across the sky when the two boys carried the last of the urns out of the furnace room. They were walking to the scribes' room, with Bartholomew in the lead carrying the top of the urn and Jotham carrying the bottom, when Bartholomew suddenly slipped. The urn went crashing to the ground and broke into thousands of pieces. Just then the Rabbi came walking across the compound and, at the sound of the crash, turned to look. Bartholomew looked back and forth between the urn and the Rabbi, his face looking like a cornered rabbit.

"Rrrabbi," he stuttered, "forgive me. I slipped in the dirt and the urn just … "

The Rabbi held up his hand to interrupt Bartholomew. He looked slowly from the broken pieces to the panic on the boy's face. "Bartholomew," he said slowly, "why are you so frightened? Is it because of the lesson you had to learn last night?"

Bartholomew nodded his head. The Rabbi grasped the boy's shoulder and said softly, "Bartholomew, the punishment you received last night was for a willful breaking of our rules. This," he said, sweeping his hand over the shattered urn, "was an accident. We do not punish men *or* boys for making mistakes. Only for acting in disobedience."

Bartholomew stopped quivering and even managed a little smile. Just then Nathan walked up. "Jotham, it is time to leave," he said. Jotham looked at Bartholomew and suddenly wasn't so sure he really wanted to leave. But then he said, "Yes, Nathan, I will gather my things."

With Bartholomew's help, Jotham gathered his new clothes, a blanket the dormitory keeper had given him, and a new food bag. Just before they left the dormitory, Bartholomew handed Jotham a walking stick. "Here," he said, "I want you to have this. It is my favorite, and it would honor me if you would use it."

Jotham stood there with his mouth open, the right words stuck somewhere behind his tongue.

"It's all right," Bartholomew said. "I have another, and you should not be traveling without one."

Jotham gave Bartholomew a long hug as he had seen his father do after successful business transactions. Then together they went and found Nathan. It was hard to walk out the front gate leaving Qumran behind. Jotham turned and gave a last wave to Bartholomew, and hoped that he would see him again someday.

"You are quiet this morning," Nathan said after a long while.

"I will miss Qumran," Jotham answered. Then a moment later added, "And Bartholomew." After some time he asked, "How far is it to Jericho?"

"Less than half the distance we traveled from En Gedi to Qumran," Nathan answered.

Jotham was pleased with this, and it lifted his spirits. They stopped to eat their noon meal among the trees and reeds at the place where the Jordan River enters the Salt Sea. Jotham had never seen such a beautiful place, and begged Nathan to let him swim in the river. "No, we must continue on," Nathan said, "if we are to reach Jericho by sundown."

All afternoon Jotham kept quizzing Nathan about Jericho. Though it was the place of his birth, Jotham really didn't know much about it.

"Will there be camel tricks there?" he asked.

"Perhaps," Nathan answered.

"What about snakes? I heard of a man who is the god of snakes and charms them with a flute. Will he be there?"

"Probably not."

Finally, Nathan was exasperated with all the questions and stopped in the middle of the road. "Jotham," he said sharply, "you really must stop asking questions about Jericho!"

"But, *Nathan*," Jotham whined, "*why?*"

"Because, my friend," Nathan said, now smiling, "we are there!"

And with that, Nathan pointed to a grove of palm trees that seemed to stick up out of the middle of the road. Beyond them, Jotham saw the city of his birth.

Jericho was even more beautiful than Jotham had remembered. Palm trees thick with dates lined the streets. All the houses were made of a reddish plaster and the roofs were brown tiles made of clay. Plants and shrubs made everything green. And everywhere Jotham looked he saw a water well. *What a rich and beautiful city*, Jotham thought. *This is where the Messiah should be born!*

Nathan led Jotham through several streets. Soon they stopped at a doorway along a narrow street and knocked on the door. A man not much taller than Jotham, but very much older, came to the door and seeing Nathan, broke into a huge grin.

"Nathan, my friend," he yelled, embracing him. "I was just thinking of you this morning!"

"And why was that? Did you break yet another pot?"

The man laughed loudly. "No such thing. I simply missed you, my friend."

They entered the house and Nathan said, "Silas, I would like you to meet my young friend, Jotham of Jericho." Then to Jotham he added, "Silas and I trained under the same Rabbi when we were young. That is, until he left the Order to make his wealth as a merchant!"

"Ah, Nathan," Silas said with a laugh, "you never miss an opportunity to twist the knife of guilt!"

"Would I inflict guilt on my best of all friends?" Nathan asked innocently. "Well, Silas," he added, "if you had not abandoned your God, I would not have this fine house to visit on my trips to Jericho."

Silas smiled a little less. "I did not abandon my God, you know. I only abandoned those who worship him in hypocrisy."

Jothan could believe that Nathan had once been young. But not so Silas. Jotham thought he looked as old as the olive trees he'd camped under. And just as wrinkled.

The three of them made their way through the house to the courtyard in the center, and here they met another man. "My friends," Silas said to Nathan and Jotham, "I would like you to meet another friend of mine. This is Hasrah of Bethlehem." They greeted each other, then all sat down on stone benches around a pond made of shiny tiles. Jotham had never seen such a place as this. He didn't much like being inside buildings—he much preferred the open spaces of the grazing meadows—but *this* house had so many colors and places to sit and trees and bushes that Jotham thought he could probably stay here for a very long time.

The three adults sat around talking for what seemed like forever to Jotham. They talked about the Romans and about Herod and about many things that Jotham didn't even understand. But when they started talking about the Messiah, Jotham's ears perked up.

"You must be excited," Nathan was saying to Hasrah, "that the Messiah shall soon come to Bethlehem."

Hasrah scoffed. "What would the *Messiah* be doing coming to such an insignificant place?"

"The Scripture is clear," Silas said, and the three men spoke of things that were now becoming familiar to Jotham.

It was well past dark when Silas finally lit some oil lamps that hung from the arches. Bored with all the talk, Jotham stood and began to explore. Several alcoves surrounded the room, and in one of those Jotham found a scroll on a pedestal. The alcove was decorated with Hebrew symbols that Jotham didn't understand. Fascinated, he gently touched the surface of the scroll.

"It's the Torah." The voice of Silas came from right behind Jotham. Jotham jumped in fright and withdrew his hand quickly.

"Do not fear," Silas said gently. "All Jehovah's children should learn to read the Torah."

Jotham looked at Silas as if the old man had just announced he could fly. "You see," Silas continued, "I am not such a bad Jew. And not so different from Nathan. I study the Torah every day, and say the prayers like any good Jew. It's just that I … I don't have much passion for some of the forms our religion takes. Or rather, some of the forms that people give it."

Jotham thought about this for a moment, then nodded, almost understanding. Then Silas turned to the rest of the group and announced in a loud voice, "My friends, let me take you for an evening meal. There is an inn down the street, and the owner is a friend of mine."

The other men agreed, and the four walked a short way down the street, which was still busy with people even after dark. They entered another building made of the same reddish plaster. As they walked through the door and into the center of the room, Jotham saw that there were many people eating at wooden tables. Hasrah let out a yell to a man at the other side of the room. "Seth!" he called out with a huge grin, "I have brought friends to meet your hospitality!"

The man had a look of panic on his face and motioned something to Hasrah, but Hasrah paid no attention. "We shall have your finest lamb and your freshest bread," he was saying. Finally Jotham looked behind him to where Seth had been gesturing.

And there, sitting at a table by the door, was Decha of Megiddo.

I will instruct you and teach you in the way you should go; I will counsel you and watch over you. Do not be like the horse or the mule, which have no understanding but must be controlled by bit and bridle, or they will not come to you. Many are the woes of the wicked, but the Lord's unfailing love surrounds the man who trusts in him. Rejoice in the Lord and be glad, you righteous; sing, all you who are upright in heart!   PSALMS 32:8-11

Bartholomew found out the difference between willful defiance and a simple mistake. And just as the Rabbi did not punish Bartholomew for his mistake, God does not punish us for ours. Like any good parent, he must discipline us when we defiantly disobey his commands, but he has a merciful heart toward us when we simply make mistakes. Or even if we purposely disobey him, but repent, as long as we have a humble heart and ask forgiveness.

As we celebrate the Christmas season, remember that there wouldn't *be* a Christmas season if it weren't for God's merciful love. Because he loves us, he has shown us mercy by sending his only Son to us. In other words, Jesus is God's response to our selfish sinful nature. Let him know today and every day that you appreciate his gift by being, yourself, merciful toward others.

Consequences

Light the first two violet candles.

Jotham's heart stopped and his mouth went dry. His knees began to shake and he felt all the blood drain from his head. Decha of Megiddo sat at the table, staring at Jotham and his companions, picking his teeth with a knife. He smiled, but it was not the smile of a friend glad to see a long lost companion. It was the smile of one who enjoyed killing, and was about to do so.

The other three men were still talking. Finally Nathan noticed the look on Jotham's face. He looked toward the door then he, too, felt the blood drain from his head. A moment later the other two men noticed and recognized Decha. They didn't know about the trouble Jotham and Nathan had barely lived through, but they did know that Decha was an evil man, and that any room he was in was not a safe room.

"Sooo," Decha said, drawing it out so that it struck the group like a bullwhip, "the fool is no fool, and tries to make a fool of Decha of Megiddo."

Nathan set his jaw and drew his shoulders up straight, but said nothing. Jotham's knees shook even harder as Decha turned toward him.

"I have followed you far, *little one*," Decha said as he stared at Jotham. "I thought I had lost you forever. But then in you walk, like a lamb to the slaughter." He threw his head back and laughed, and it sounded to Jotham like the roar of a lion and the laugh of a hyena put together.

Silas the merchant and Hasrah of Bethlehem stepped up beside Nathan, ready to join him in whatever was to come. As Decha's attention was on Jotham, Nathan whispered, "Hasrah! When the fighting starts, take Jotham and run!"

"Friend, you are outnumbered. I cannot leave you to fight alone."

Hasrah was right, of course. Decha had four tall men with him, each with muscles that looked to Jotham like the trunks of trees, and swords that were longer than Jotham was tall.

"No," Nathan hissed, "save the boy! There is a priest Zechariah who lives in the hills to the north. Take the boy there. He will be safe."

Hasrah didn't like the idea of leaving his friends to fight five bigger men, but knew he must honor Nathan's wishes.

"Very well," he whispered. "I shall take care of the boy. Jehovah be with you!"

Suddenly Decha turned his attention to Nathan. "And you, fool," he spat, drawing his curved sword, "it is you who *stole* my prize, and for that you must die!"

Decha's sword sliced through the air directly at Nathan's stomach, but Nathan jumped aside. Grabbing a chair he swung at Decha's arm, knocking the sword from his hand. Silas, too, took up a chair just as Decha's four men jumped up and drew their own swords. In that same moment Hasrah swept Jotham into his arms and headed for the back of the inn, calling on the innkeeper to help his friends. Jotham kicked and screamed at Hasrah to let him go help Nathan, but Hasrah held tight.

Decha screamed in pain and anger. He picked up his sword and began hacking at the chair Nathan held up in defense.

The other four men had surrounded Silas, blocking Jotham's view. In a moment that was burned into Jotham's memory forever, he watched as two of the men drew their swords. A moment later Silas fell to the ground in a heap and didn't move.

Jotham screamed, and watched the four men surround Nathan. Just as he and Hasrah slammed through the door and out into the night, Nathan looked Jotham square in the eye and mouthed one word. "Shalom," he said, which means "Peace." Then the door slammed shut just as a long, curved sword sliced through the air directly at Nathan's neck. Everything went black as Hasrah carried Jotham into the night, with Jotham still screaming.

"Quiet, I bid you, young one," whispered Hasrah. "These streets are not friendly in the night!"

They ran to the back of Silas' house where Hasrah's camel was tethered. Quickly they untied and mounted the beast. With two clicks of his tongue and a jab in the ribs with his heels, Hasrah spurred the animal to full speed. Down the streets of Jericho they raced, and out into the black desert night.

Jotham clutched Hasrah with all his strength as he sobbed into the back of Hasrah's tunic. "Peace, my son," Hasrah called back. "The angels of Jehovah are with our friends now."

Just outside Jericho, Hasrah left the road and shot straight up into the hills. The moon had not yet risen, and all Jotham could see was blackness. He could not even see the ground under the camel's feet. "How can you see where you're going?" Jotham cried, fear of being thrown to the ground overtaking his grief at what he had just witnessed.

"Fear not, my friend," Hasrah answered over the pounding of camel hooves. "In my younger days my friends and I raided the Roman camps outside Jericho. I have navigated these back trails on many dark nights."

Jotham's bottom was getting sore from all the bouncing by the time Hasrah finally slowed the camel to a walk. The camel heaved huge breaths, and Jotham thought it smelled a lot like a particular meal his mother made—a meal that caused even the sheep to run away. "I believe we are safe now," Hasrah said. They had climbed far into the hills and were now on top of a plateau. The wind blew hard, here, and would cover up their tracks the moment they were made.

As they travelled on, Jotham began to breathe easier and his heart slowed down a bit. That's when the grief fully struck him, and he began to sob once again.

"I killed them," he cried, "I killed them both."

Hasrah stopped the camel and lifted Jotham to the ground, shielding him from the wind and sand. "Jotham, Jotham, what are you saying? You have killed *no one*. It was Decha, that beast." Hasrah spit on the ground after speaking the name of Decha. "May Jehovah reward him richly for this deed!"

"No, it was *me*," Jotham cried. "Don't you *see*? If it weren't for me, Nathan and Silas would still be alive!"

Hasrah hugged Jotham close. "Here now, boy, you must not believe such things. Decha alone is responsible for this evil!"

Jotham didn't say anything, but deep in his heart he knew that all of this started the morning he had disobeyed his father.

After a few minutes, Hasrah lifted Jotham back onto the camel and together they rode through the night. It was just before dawn when they approached a small group of clay houses with a well in front. As they approached, a tall, thin man with long grey hair came from one house, holding a lamp up in front of him. Through sleepy eyes, Jotham saw that he looked as old as Moses himself. "Who is that?" the man shouted. "Who's there?"

"Shalom, friend," Hasrah shouted back. "It is a weary traveler and a small boy. We seek refuge from marauders!"

"Do I know this one who calls me friend?"

"No, you do not. But we are sent by Nathan of Qumran. Would you be the priest Zechariah?"

"I would indeed! And if you be sent of Nathan, you truly are my friend. Come now, and tell me of marauders!"

Quickly they all went inside the house where Zechariah's wife, Elizabeth, was waiting in her night clothes. Hasrah gently set Jotham down at a table where he was instantly asleep. A few minutes later, Hasrah had explained all about Silas, Nathan, and the boy.

"What is Decha doing this far south?" Zechariah asked no one in particular. Then he looked at Jotham with compassion. "Of course, we will be glad to hide the boy here until his family can be found."

Hasrah gently shook Jotham awake. "Jotham," he said, "this is Zechariah. He is a priest and will take care of you for a few days. I must return to my inn at Bethlehem, but I shall keep my eyes searching for your family."

Jotham nodded. He had met so many people since leaving his family that he didn't think he had any more friendship to give. And now here was one more he had to part from. But he hugged Hasrah tightly, then greeted Zechariah politely.

"And this is my little family," Zechariah said proudly. Jotham was amazed when the old man pointed to an equally old woman who was holding a brand new baby. "This is my wife Elizabeth," he said. "And this is my new son. His name is John."

And so Jotham began another night away from his family, and another night with strangers. As he looked out the window from his makeshift bed, he stared at the stars and thought about Nathan. And about the terrible consequences of disobedience. He looked at his mother's star once more, the one that shined brighter than any other, and wondered if anything would ever be the same again.

Throughout the Bible we read story after story about the terrible consequences of sin. Adam and Eve were thrown out of the Garden, the entire world was destroyed by a flood, David committed adultery, and the son born to him died because of it. Sin has consequence, sometimes even after we're forgiven.

Jotham is sad today, sad at losing Nathan and Silas, and sad that he is partly to blame. It's much more fun to think of happy things during Advent, but we must remember that the world Jesus entered was and is a cruel and evil world.

Learning that there are consequences for our sin is not very pleasant. Like Jotham, we sometimes don't understand this until we have done something that hurts someone else terribly. But then, that was exactly why Jesus came to earth, to bring us forgiveness for our disobedience, and to teach us how to love each other and obey those in authority over us.

Yes, Christmas is a happy time. But it is happy because God loved us enough to save us from our own selfishness. He came to show us that even when we must suffer the *consequences* of our actions, there is still hope and forgiveness through Jesus.

Prepare the Way

Light the first two violet candles.

Jotham woke to the sound of a crying baby. Elizabeth had made him a bed in front of the fire, but even the warmth of the flames didn't help him sleep well. Between the baby's crying and dreams of Nathan, he'd tossed and turned much of the night.

And now here he was, once again waking up in a strange place with people he'd only just met. *Will I ever see my family again?* he wondered. He longed to hug his mother and to tell his father he was sorry. He actually looked forward to the punishment his father would give him! *If only I could find him,* Jotham thought.

"Good morning," came a soft voice. It was the woman of the house—was it Esther?... no, Elizabeth, that was it!

"Good morning," Jotham answered. She was much older than his mother, he saw, but was nursing a baby. *How can that be?* he wondered. He had only seen young girls with babies.

"The peace of Jehovah be with you, Jotham. You have nothing to fear here. You are among friends. As soon as John has had his breakfast," she said, nodding toward the baby in her arms, "I will bake you some parched corn."

Elizabeth's gentle words eased some of the loneliness he was feeling, and the thought of roasted heads of corn made his mouth water. "It is kind of you to care for me," he said. "Do you think Decha of Megiddo will find me here?"

"I do not believe so," she answered. "We are very far from Jericho, and his caravan has never passed this way before."

Elizabeth finished feeding the baby, then gave him to Jotham to hold. Jotham liked the feel of the baby in his arms, and it made him happy when the child grabbed tightly onto his nose. "He's very strong," he said to Elizabeth.

"Yes, he is. And he shall have to be for the task which lies ahead of him."

Jotham scrunched up his face, confused. "What task could a little baby have?" he asked.

Elizabeth smiled. "This is a very special baby, Jotham. Perhaps you should go and ask Zechariah about him while I roast your corn."

"May I take John with me?"

"Of course, but be careful to hold his head up as I showed you."

Jotham carefully walked outside and found Zechariah sawing firewood. After giving the proper greetings he said, "Elizabeth told me that John is a special baby and that you would tell me why."

Zechariah laughed. "Oh, she *did*, did she? Well then, I guess I must tell my story yet again." He motioned for Jotham to sit on a log, then did the same himself. He reached over to tickle John's chin, and as he did, Jotham realized for the first time just how many wrinkles the baby's father had.

"I am a priest of the division of Abijah," Zechariah started, "eighth among the divisions of priests. About a year ago my division was on duty in the temple in Jerusalem, and I was chosen by lot to enter the Holy Place to burn the incense before the Lord." Jotham noticed that Zechariah seemed to be gazing off into the sky now, and his voice became very quiet. "I had just lit the incense," he continued, "when a bright light appeared to the right of the altar. It was a thousand times brighter than the sun, yet I could look at it. And it was beautiful! Oh, so beautiful."

Jotham could barely hear the old man's words now. He leaned forward so as not to miss a syllable. Then Zechariah looked straight into Jotham's eyes and said loudly, "It was an angel! An *angel*," he repeated. "Coming to visit *me!* 'Do not be afraid, Zechariah,' he said. 'Your prayer has been heard. Your wife Elizabeth will bear you a son, and you are to give him the name John. He will be a joy and a delight to you, and many will rejoice because of his birth for he will be great in the sight of the Lord. He is never to take wine or other fermented drink,' the angel said. 'And he will be filled with the Holy Spirit even from birth. He will bring many of the people of Israel back to the Lord their God. And he will go on before the Lord in the spirit and power of Elijah to turn the hearts of the fathers to their children and the disobedient to the wisdom of the righteous.'" Here Zechariah grabbed Jotham's arm and said, "'To make ready a people prepared for the Lord!'"

Zechariah was breathing hard now, excited at reliving the visit of the angel. "It was a wondrous sight, Jotham," he said, standing and pacing. "And such wondrous words! But I am an old man! My wife and I have wanted a child for fifty years, but always she is barren. Yet this angel is telling me that we will have a child in our old age!" Zechariah almost shouted at Jotham, "Is it any wonder that I doubted those words?"

The old man calmed down again, sat on the log, and slowly shook his head. "But I *did* doubt, and because of it, the angel said, 'I am Gabriel. I stand in the presence of God and I have been sent to speak to you and to tell you this good news. And now you will be silent and not able to speak until the day this happens because you did not believe my words that will come true at their proper time.' And so my mouth was closed and I was unable to speak until the eighth day after the child's birth."

Jotham sat staring, transfixed by the story the old man told. He barely breathed, and tried to open his ears wide so as not to miss a word. Never before had he heard such a tale from someone who had actually been visited by an angel!

"On that day," Zechariah concluded, "my family wanted to name the boy after me. But I wrote on a tablet, 'No! He is to be called John!' And at that moment, my mouth was opened again, and I spent many hours praising God."

Jotham looked at the baby in his arms and wondered how it could be that such a small child would bring people back to Jehovah. "How will all this happen?" he asked. "How is it that John will do all this?"

Zechariah looked up, almost as if he hadn't realized Jotham was there. "That is quite simple, Jotham," he said quietly. Then looking at his son in Jotham's arms he said, "John is here to prepare the way of the Messiah."

"But *how?*" Jotham pleaded. "How will he prepare the way of the Messiah when the Messiah hasn't appeared yet!?"

The old man stood and began sawing his wood once again. "For that," he said, "you had better talk to my wife."

As Jotham carried the baby back to the house, the child grabbed Jotham's nose and held on tightly, laughing. Inside, Elizabeth was just finishing up making some bread dough.

"Elizabeth," Jotham said, pulling John's hand from his nose, "Zechariah said you would tell me how John will prepare the way of the Messiah."

Elizabeth eyed Jotham as if trying to decide if he could understand what she was about to tell him. Finally she decided in his favor and, after wiping her hands and sitting down at the table, she told him everything. "It all started," she said, "with a visit from my cousin, Mary … "

A voice of one calling: "In the desert prepare the way for the LORD; make straight in the wilderness a highway for our God" (Is 40:3).

Seven hundred years before John the Baptist was born, this prophecy in Isaiah told how he would come and wander in the desert to announce the arrival of the Messiah. God wanted there to be no mistake that the Messiah was coming, and so sent John before him to "prepare the way."

Today, God sends his Holy Spirit to prepare our hearts for receiving the good news of salvation. Even before we ever heard the name of Jesus, his Spirit was in us, testifying to us of his great love. God wants to be sure that every soul has an opportunity to know him personally.

Advent is a time of looking forward, of preparing the way. Each of us should take this time to examine our hearts, to see if we're truly ready for the celebration of Christ's birth. God has prepared our hearts to understand and accept his Christmas message of unfailing mercy and unselfish love. We'll know we're *ready* for Christmas when we start living that message in our actions toward others.

Revelation

Light the first two violet candles.

The aroma of the parched corn drifted across the table and made Jotham's mouth water. He had never figured out why they called it "parched corn" when it was really roasted heads of wheat, but they tasted so good they could call it anything they wanted, he decided. He popped one of the heads in his mouth and the toasted grain surrounded his taste buds with its nutty flavor.

"My cousin, Mary, is much younger than I, and lives a far distance from here," Elizabeth continued, still kneading the bread with her knuckles. "She came to visit me about six months after I became pregnant with John. I didn't even know she was coming. But Mary and I have always been very close. She knew she was welcome at any time. Would you like some milk, Jotham?"

Jotham nodded his head, and Elizabeth poured him a cup of goat's milk from a leather pouch hanging on the wall. The fresh milk washed down the grains of wheat, and Jotham thought that nothing much in the world could taste any better.

"Well anyhow," Elizabeth said, hanging the milk bag back on the wall, "I was kneading some dough one afternoon, just like now, when I heard Mary's voice greeting me as she came through the door. Immediately the baby inside me—John—began kicking and jumping until I thought I was going to be sick to my stomach! It was as if he was all excited at seeing Mary and wanted to get out and greet her."

Elizabeth slammed the dough hard against the table and Jotham's cup of milk jumped. "Finally the child inside me settled down," she continued, "and I gave Mary a proper greeting. It was only then I learned that she was also going to have a child. Well! You can imagine my joy. But all of a sudden," and here Elizabeth stopped kneading the dough and stared ahead with a dazed look, just like Zechariah had, "all of a sudden, I was speaking words that I hadn't thought of. 'Blessed are you among women,' I said, 'and blessed is the child you will bear.' And in that moment I *knew,*" she said, looking at Jotham again. "I don't know how, but I just knew … "

Elizabeth's voice trailed off and her eyes were glazed again. "Knew *what?*" Jotham said finally.

"I knew," Elizabeth continued, "that my cousin Mary was to be the mother of the Messiah!"

Jotham almost fell from the bench. He dropped the head of wheat he was about to munch and gasped, "She was *what?*"

"The mother of the Messiah."

Jotham's head spun. It had been hard for him to believe Nathan when he said that the Messiah could come sometime during Jotham's life, or that he was going to be born like any other baby. But to hear that the Messiah was already on his way, that he had a real mother with a real name, and that that mother had been in this very house … well, it just made Jotham's insides wiggle with excitement like a bowl of worms. And this woman sitting in front of me, Jotham thought, actually *knows* the mother of the Messiah!

"How do you know she is pregnant with the Messiah?" he asked finally. Elizabeth smiled.

"Well, Mary told me that one day an angel of the Lord appeared to her and told her she would give birth to a son because God's Spirit would come upon her. The angel even told her what to name the child." Elizabeth started kneading the bread dough again as she talked. "Mary said that within a few days after the angel's visit she discovered she was, indeed, going to have a baby. And oh what a stir *that* caused. Everyone knew she was not yet married, and her fiance wanted nothing to do with her. But something happened and all of a sudden he changed his mind and, well, anyhow, she's going to have a baby."

Jotham put his chin on the table to rest his head. He felt weak all over. Even his earlobes felt heavy. Angels! How could that be? He'd heard of them, of course, but that was always in *stories*, and in Scripture. Nobody in *modern* times really talked to angels, he knew.

"What was the name?" Jotham whispered hoarsely after several minutes.

"What was *who's* name?"

"The baby—the Messiah. What was the name the angel said to give him?"

"Oh that," Elizabeth said. "It was Jesus. The angel said to name the boy Jesus."

Jotham spent all that afternoon stacking Zechariah's firewood and thinking. There were so many thoughts swirling around in his brain that he felt like he needed *two* heads just to think them all. In one of his heads, he decided, he'd just think about his family. Where could they be by now? What were his brothers doing? Had they ever gone to Hebron? He imagined seeing them tending to their sheep. He imagined seeing his father sitting cross-legged in his tent making a business deal with another sheepherder. He imagined helping his mother make bread cakes and listening to her hum his favorite songs.

With my other head, Jotham thought, *I'll think about the Messiah.* The news he'd heard about the Messiah since he'd been parted from his family seemed like a dream. *Could it possibly be true,* he wondered? For centuries, Jotham knew, his people had been waiting for the Messiah King to ride through all of Palestine defeating the Babylonians and Romans and anyone else that didn't treat God's chosen ones properly. But the Scriptures read to him by Eliakim the shepherd and Nathan the teacher seemed to say that the Messiah would come as a baby, to suffer and die for the sins of the world.

And then what Zechariah and Elizabeth had told him today! Well now, *there* was an incredible story!

But I guess I need a third head, too, Jotham finally decided. *One just to think about Nathan, and Silas, and how much I miss them.*

Late in the afternoon a windstorm blew across the plateau. Grains of sand propelled by the wind stung Jotham's arms and legs, and finally he and Zechariah ran to the house for cover. He brushed himself off inside the door, then shook his hair like a dog to get the sand out.

"I hope my family is camped in a good place," he said. "The wind is strong enough to carry away even my father's tent!"

"No doubt they are well," Zechariah said. "I'm sure your father is a wise and experienced man. Why don't you tell me about him?"

Jotham's heart leaped for joy at the prospect of talking about his father. He pulled John onto his lap, then began. "He comes from the area of Jerusalem, from the house of David. He had seven brothers," Jotham said, repeating what he'd been taught many times, "most of them shepherds like him. But one brother was taken by Roman soldiers to be a slave, and one is a merchant or something."

The wind was howling outside now, and Zechariah lit a lamp as darkness crept through the windows.

"His youngest brother is a carpenter in a place called Nazareth," Jotham continued, rocking John in his arms, "but I've never met him."

Suddenly Jotham noticed that Zechariah and Elizabeth had both stopped what they were doing and were staring at him, their eyes wide open. "What is your uncle's name?" Zechariah finally whispered.

Jotham looked at them as if they had suddenly been taken with Mad Camel disease. "Which uncle?" he asked.

"The young one—the one in Nazareth," Zechariah wheezed.

"Oh," Jotham said plainly. "His name is Joseph."

Elizabeth sat down on the bench with a big thud and put one hand to her cheek as if she had just seen an angel herself. "Jotham," she said quietly, "your uncle is the earthly father of the Messiah—the one God has put in charge to take care of the baby and his mother."

In some places in the world people think it's very important to know who your ancestors are. People will treat you differently depending on who your great, great, great grandfather was, or where your family came from. Imagine then, how it would feel to be told you were a direct relative of Mary or Joseph.

For Jotham, it's almost too hard to think about. It seems impossibly wondrous that one so insignificant as he could be related to Jesus. It kind of left him speechless. But Mary expressed it well when she discovered she was to be the *mother* of the Messiah. She said, "My soul praises the Lord, and my spirit rejoices in God my Savior!"

So how would *you* feel? How would you feel if you discovered tomorrow that Jesus is your brother? He is, of course, if you've chosen to be adopted into his family. He's as real a brother as any human boy could ever be. And this means that *his* Father is *your* father as well.

Doesn't that make Christmas a bit more meaningful? It's not just another birthday, it's your *brother's* birthday!

Shall we celebrate?

Ways and Means

Light the first two violet candles.

For every star he saw through the window, Jotham made one imaginary mark on his leg with his finger. It was the only way he knew to count, and he'd seen his father do it many times in the dirt as they counted their sheep.

He'd been lying there for hours, trying to sleep, but nothing could keep his mind from thinking about the fact that the Messiah was going to be his cousin! Between that and the wind that still blew outside, Jotham hadn't slept a moment.

Sometime after midnight, Jotham saw the same bright star he'd been watching since he was parted from his family. Just like before, he wondered if maybe his mother was looking at the same star. She could be, he knew, because no matter where you travelled, you could always see the same stars. The thought gave him comfort, and a short time later he was finally asleep.

After breakfast the next morning, Jotham took care of John so Elizabeth could talk with Zechariah. Jotham liked playing with the baby. It made him feel more grown up.

Nothing much went on all morning and Jotham was becoming bored. Once, a rider came through and asked if he could water his horse, and Jotham was sure Zechariah wouldn't mind so had let him. Other than that, he just played with John and wondered where the wind had gone to when it ceased blowing earlier that morning. *Is it all stored in a cave somewhere?* Jotham wondered.

Just before lunch Zechariah called Jotham in. "We've been talking," he said, waving his hand to three other men and Elizabeth, "and we believe we may know where your family is."

Jotham jumped up, almost dropping John on his head. Elizabeth grabbed the baby as Jotham said, "Where? Where?"

"Easy, Jotham, we are not at all certain of this. First, let me ask you some questions. Did your father say anything in the last few weeks about returning to the place of his birth?"

Jotham shrugged. "I don't know. He and my mother talk about many things. Mostly I don't listen."

Zechariah frowned. "Well, did he say anything at all about traveling?"

"I don't know," Jotham said again, and this frustrated the men.

"But you said he was sending your brothers to the city. Did he say why?"

At this Jotham's face lit up, because he finally knew an answer. "Yes! He told my brothers to sell a tenth of their sheep to a man there."

Zechariah sat back and slapped the table. "That's it, then," he said. "It must be."

Jotham looked from face to face trying to figure out what they were talking about. "*What's* it?" he pleaded. "*What* must be?"

Zechariah looked at Jotham and then slowly said, "Your father is headed to the place of his birth for the census."

Jotham stared, not understanding. "What's a census?" he asked.

"A census is when the government counts all the people under its rule," one of the other men said. "Each family must return to the place of the father's birth to be counted and pay tax."

"Which is why," Zechariah added, "your father is going there. If he told your brothers to sell a tenth of their flock, it must have been so he could pay his taxes."

Suddenly it all became clear to Jotham and he jumped up, finally excited. "That means my father is on his way to Jerusalem!"

"Exactly. Unless he's already been there and left again. He's had more than a week, and could easily travel that far in that time."

"Then I've got to go right *now!*" Jotham yelled, not caring for a moment who had authority over him.

"I had a feeling you might say that," Zechariah said. "So we've been talking, and it's been decided that Caleb here shall take you to Jerusalem." He pointed to a man that Jotham thought didn't look much older than his oldest brother. "It will be a long, hard journey, but not so far as you've already come. I would take you myself, but I am old and Caleb will serve you better."

"I am honored for the kindness you show to a simple sheepherder," Jotham said with a bow, repeating another of his father's sayings. He didn't notice that the adults all looked at each other and smiled.

"We leave tomorrow at first light," Caleb announced, and Jotham's heart fell.

"Can't we leave *today?*" he asked. "My father might even now be packing his tents!"

"Jotham, it is not polite to receive a gift and then ask for more," Elizabeth scolded. "Be thankful that Caleb has agreed to this journey at all."

"Forgive me," Jotham said, frustrated. "It's just that I've been away from my family for a very long time."

"I understand," Caleb said, "and we would leave immediately if it were at all possible. But I'm afraid that it is not. We have much packing to do, and I must prepare the animals for the journey."

Jotham nodded glumly but didn't say anything. He knew Caleb was doing his best, but he still wished there was some way to leave right now.

Caleb went to the stable to feed and water the donkeys, and Jotham went to help him. Caleb was nice, he decided, and he looked forward to their trip together.

Having done all he could do to help Caleb, Jotham decided to make the afternoon go quicker by stacking the firewood left over from the day before. As he did, he dreamed of arriving in Jerusalem and finding his family there. He planned out just what he would say to his father, and just how hard he would hug his mother. She would cry, he decided, since she thought he was dead and didn't expect to see him.

Jotham was just finishing up the wood when thunder began rolling in from the west. Another storm, he thought, and he hoped it wouldn't delay their trip. He could see that Caleb was packing bedding and food into the saddle bags that would go on the donkeys. Then he watched as Caleb crossed to the house, and thought again what a good friend he was going to make.

The thunder was getting closer and louder, and Jotham decided he'd better hurry and get the wood stacked. He turned back to his work and was thinking so hard that he didn't even notice that the thunder didn't sound much like thunder any more. And when finally it grew so loud that he turned to face the storm, he faced instead the sight of a dozen horses at a full run, headed straight for him.

And leading them all, on a horse that looked like the devil himself, was Decha of Megiddo.

Decha didn't take his eyes off Jotham, but just whipped his horse to go faster. Jotham couldn't make his muscles move, and just stood there in shock. Then Decha rode right past him, never taking his eyes off Jotham. Suddenly Jotham felt himself lifted from the ground by two pairs of powerful hands. He was being swept away between two gigantic horses, held there in midair by two of Decha's men. Zechariah and the other men ran from the house just in time to see the horsemen and Jotham disappearing over the hill.

The man on Jotham's left threw him roughly across his lap so that Jotham was lying on his stomach. Every bounce of the horse slammed his stomach into the rider's knees, and the ground whisked by at a dizzying speed. Within minutes Jotham became sick and wretched up all the parched corn that Elizabeth had so lovingly made him.

But worse than any of this, worse even than the fact that he had been taken by Decha of Megiddo, was the fact that they were riding east.

Away from Jerusalem.

For my thoughts are not your thoughts, neither are your ways my ways, declares the Lord. As the heavens are higher than the earth, so are my ways higher than your ways and my thoughts than your thoughts.   ISAIAH 55:8

Joseph must have wondered why, of all the times for there to be a census, they had to pick the time when his baby was due to be born. If God was so involved in this birth, Joseph might have wondered, why did he allow the government to call for a census just then?

But, of course, if Joseph and Mary hadn't been forced to travel to Bethlehem, then the prophecy about the birthplace of the Messiah would never have been fulfilled. Nor would the prophecy about there being no room in the inn, or about Jesus lying in the manger. What may have seemed like a mistake to Joseph was actually just God's way of carrying out his plan.

Jotham feels like his whole world has just fallen apart. Not only is his life in danger, but he's traveling farther and farther from his family. Surely, this can't be God's way of working things out, can it? As we watch the seemingly accidental events of our Christmas story unfold, maybe we should look back on our *own* lives, and see if we can't recognize some "ways" which were not ours, but God's.

Rescue in the Night

Light two violet candles and the pink candle.

Jotham's eyeballs were going to pop out, he was sure. He felt as if all the blood in his body had gathered behind his eyeballs as he lay across the lap of Decha's horseman. The constant bouncing knocked the wind out of him, and with every breath it seemed as if a bear was crushing him with a death-hug. He had long ago retched up any food that was in his stomach, and the wind created by the running horse made his arms and legs feel as cold as he could ever remember being.

The dozen riders were heading east. *I wonder if we're going back to Jericho,* Jotham thought. But mostly he just wondered if his body would split in half across the horse before they got to where they were going.

Just when Jotham thought he'd be smothered by sweaty horse hair, the horses finally slowed. They circled around a small watering hole and stopped, panting hard. The twelve riders jumped off their horses and stretched. A man pulled Jotham off the horse and he fell in a heap on the ground.

The man laughed.

Jotham lay there feeling as if he'd been run over by a herd of camels. Every muscle ached, and his head felt as if it was full of kicking donkeys. He tried to pretend that none of this was real, that it hadn't really happened. But then he felt a toe in his side and an irresistible force pushed him over onto his back. He was looking straight up into the face of Decha, who had one arm in a sling.

"Well, *little one*," he sneered. "Finally you are mine!" He laughed that laugh that Jotham hated so much, the one that made Jotham's stomach feel hollow. "Of course, I didn't realize who you were, or I never would have let you go." He laughed again, long and loud, then all of a sudden dropped to one knee and put his sword to Jotham's throat with his good hand. "Where is your Jehovah *now*, little one?" he hissed, and the stench of his breath made Jotham gag. "You see, he is not here. Pray to your Jehovah if you wish, but remember it is *I* who will decide if you live or die!"

Decha drew the sword across Jotham's throat, and Jotham felt the edge of the blade tickle his skin. Then Decha smiled, and Jotham saw that most his teeth were black with rot, and his breath smelled like the dung gate at En Gedi.

"But no," he said after a moment, "I won't kill you just yet. You have something I want."

"I … I have nothing!" Jotham cried.

"No, but you know where it is. And you will tell me," Decha said, laying the sword against Jotham's cheek, "or I shall cut out your tongue."

Just then one of Decha's men shouted something and Decha jumped to his feet. He stared into the west, toward the setting sun, the direction they had come from. Jotham sat up too, and saw a cloud of dust near the horizon.

"They're following us, the fools," Decha said.

Caleb, no, Jotham thought. *Go back! They'll kill you!*

"You three," Decha yelled to three men sitting at the edge of the water hole. "Go kill whoever follows us, then meet us at the hanging tree."

Immediately the three jumped to their feet and onto their horses. With war yells that stabbed a knife of fright through Jotham's heart, the three kicked their horses hard and rode off in the direction of the dust cloud.

Yes, Jehovah, I pray to you, Jotham thought. *I pray that you will protect my friends. I shall make whatever offering I can whenever I can, if you will just do this one thing for me!*

Decha now ordered the rest of the men to mount, and Jotham felt himself lifted to his feet. "Lodan," the man he had been riding with called to another, "take this boy. I'm tired of him."

A punch in Jotham's back threw him over toward the other man. Jotham tripped and fell at the man's feet. With a sigh of disgust, Lodan threw Jotham across the horse then climbed up behind him. *This man smells even worse than the other,* Jotham decided, *but at least he's letting me sit up.*

Being upright didn't help Jotham's stomach much, as they now left the plateau and dropped slowly down through jagged ravines. Jotham was thrown from one side to the other as the horse searched for footing among the rocks. In some places the path was so steep that he felt as if he would fall straight down over the horse's head.

The sun had set by the time they reached the bottom and the ground leveled out. The half-moon gave off a little bit of light, but Jotham still couldn't see very far ahead. Once again the riders dismounted, then tied Jotham to a tall, bare tree. They seemed to be waiting for something, and Jotham figured it must be the three men Decha had sent out. When they returned, he knew it would mean that Caleb and the others were dead.

But they didn't return.

Most of the nine men fell asleep. A few munched on bread crusts. Decha paced between a log and a rock, his sword glinting off the moonlight each time he reversed direction at the log. But still, the men did not return.

Finally, in anger, Decha began yelling and kicking at the sleeping men. At that three of them mounted their horses and headed back up the trail, riding as fast as they could through the jagged rocks.

Decha began pacing again and soon ordered everyone else onto their horses. The men quickly gathered their blankets and food and mounted up. Lodan pulled Jotham up by the neck of his tunic. They rode ahead until they came to a grove of olive trees, where they circled the horses in close and tied up Jotham again. The men used their horses as shields against whatever enemy might be approaching. The men were getting nervous, Jotham could see, and Decha was yelling and kicking more than ever.

"You are a devil," Decha hissed, and the sudden sound behind his head sent spiders up Jotham's neck. "You have brought nothing but anger to my heart, and *pain* to my body," he said, raising his injured arm. "Well, *no more!* Tomorrow you will lead me where I want to go and then I shall kill you!"

Decha didn't laugh this time, and even though his threats made Jotham's heart jump, he also thought he saw something else in Decha's face. He thought he saw … fear.

The hours passed and Jotham watched the moon trek across the sky. The night was quiet, except for Decha's pacing. He still yelled at the men, but he did it in a whisper that sounded like a snake hissing. He made all the men stay awake and stand in a circle beside their horses. Each man had his sword drawn and searched the darkness for any sign of movement. Jotham was still tied to an olive tree.

Decha continued to pace, stopping every few seconds to look up the trail. *Six men have left to kill Caleb,* Jotham thought. *And six men have not returned.*

As the moon drifted down over the hills, Jotham's eyes finally became too heavy to hold open. He leaned his head back against the rough bark of the olive tree. His mouth was parched, his stomach was empty, but still, sleep climbed under his eyelids within seconds.

The next thing Jotham knew, a hand was clamped over his mouth from behind. The hand was cutting off Jotham's air, smothering him. He kicked and jumped as much as he could tied to the tree, but the hand held tight, and Jotham felt himself panic as the last of the air in his lungs seemed to burn through his chest. Decha had finally gone mad, Jotham realized, and was killing him out of pure hate.

"Jotham!" a voice behind him hissed, "stop moving! And don't cry out, or I'll have to keep your mouth covered!"

And suddenly Jotham became very still, the thrill of a thousand camel races exploding inside him. Because he recognized the voice he heard. It was the voice of Nathan.

"Praise be to the Lord, to God our Savior, who daily bears our burdens. Our God is a God who saves; from the Sovereign Lord comes escape from death" (Ps 68:19-20).

At just the right moment, Nathan showed up quite unexpectedly to save Jotham.

At just the right moment, God sent Jesus quite unexpectedly to save us from our selfishness.

Now we must each decide what to do with our salvation. Jotham *could* jump up, yell to Decha that he was being rescued, and thus invite Decha to come and kill him. Or, he can quietly slip away unnoticed.

Each of *us* have the choice to brag and act selfishly, and thus invite Satan to come in and destroy our lives. Or, we can quietly live our lives as Jesus did, caring more about others than about ourselves.

Jotham is lucky that Nathan is not selfish and unforgiving. *We* are lucky that *God* is not selfish and unforgiving. Can we then act toward others as God has acted toward us?

Sanctity

Light two violet candles and the pink candle.

Jotham's head spun with questions. How could Nathan be alive? How did he get here? Why would he risk his life to *save* Jotham? How would they escape?

A moment later the rope that bound Jotham's hands fell loose and he rubbed his wrists gratefully. Then, strong arms lifted him off the ground and carried him swiftly into the olive trees, away from Decha's camp. A safe distance away, Jotham was set gently down, and he found himself looking at the smiling face of Nathan. "It is good to see you, small one," Nathan said.

Jotham still couldn't believe his eyes. He hugged Nathan tightly and began to cry. "I thought Decha killed you," he sobbed. "I thought *I* killed you!"

"As you can see, it is not true."

"But I saw Silas … "

"Shh! Shh! small one, I know. Our friend Silas has gone to be with Jehovah." Then Nathan held Jotham at arm's length and said, "But we are alive, and I think we should stay that way!"

Jotham smiled a little, then Nathan picked him up once again and slid quietly through the trees. "How did you get away from Decha?" Jotham whispered.

"The innkeeper—the friend of Hasrah's—came to my aid along with seven other big men that were at the inn. They drove Decha off, then I slipped out of Jericho in the darkness. I have been traveling to Zechariah's house ever since, but it is slow going on foot through these hills."

Nathan ducked down behind a large rock and held Jotham tight. "I came across Caleb on the trail this afternoon and he told me what had happened. That's when we made our plan."

"*What* plan?" Jotham asked excitedly.

Just then the clatter of metal against metal and men screaming drifted through the trees.

"*That* plan," Nathan said, hanging his head. "May Jehovah be with them."

Jotham gave a little shudder at the sounds of men dying, and Nathan held him even closer. After a few minutes the sounds stopped and Nathan stood. "Come, Jotham, let us see the fate of our friends."

"But, Nathan, won't they *kill* us?" Jotham cried.

"Won't *who* kill us, small one?"

"*Decha's men!*"

Nathan kept walking, leading Jotham by the hand. "Decha's men are dead," he said flatly.

"But how can you *know?*"

"Because if Decha had won," Nathan said with just a touch of sorrow, "he would be celebrating loudly. Since it is quiet," he listened for a moment before finishing, "we know that our friends have killed Decha and are in mourning."

"Why mourn for *that* camel dung?" Jotham spat. Nathan stopped walking and dropped to one knee, facing the boy.

"Jotham, it is a terrible thing to take the life of another, even when it is necessary. Decha and his men are Jehovah's children, even if they don't act like it. To take their lives was a sad and difficult thing. Caleb mourns that it was a necessary thing to do."

Jotham nodded his head slowly. He didn't quite understand how someone like Decha could be one of Jehovah's chosen ones, but he could see that Nathan believed very deeply in what he was saying, and Jotham trusted anything that Nathan said.

Within minutes they arrived back at the place where Jotham had been held captive only a short time before. A fire had been built, and Jotham could see by its light the bodies of Decha's men lying in a row, blood oozing from their chests. As Nathan had predicted, Caleb and his men knelt around the bodies, their heads bowed in reverent silence. Finally, Caleb spoke.

"Jehovah, forgive your servants," he said softly, "for what we have had to do on this night. Judge the spirits of these men as you will, and judge us in light of your mercy."

All the men said, "Selah," then they stood and, one by one, threw the bodies into the flames. As his men did this, Caleb came over to Jotham and clamped his hands on Jotham's shoulders. "It is good to see you alive," he said with a smile.

Jotham hugged him with the strength of a bear cub. "Thank you," he said, sobbing. He now understood what Nathan had been saying.

"Decha and two of his men escaped," Caleb said to Nathan. "But we have their horses. They are on foot."

Nathan thought for a moment. "I think it best if Jotham and I ride to Jericho," he said. "The boy will be safer there."

It was late that night when Jotham and Nathan arrived back in Jericho. Caleb and his band were camped at the site of the battle and would return to Zechariah in the morning. Nathan and Jotham made their way to Silas' house.

The house was empty without Silas, but Jotham was so exhausted that he was instantly asleep. The next morning the sun rose bright and warm, and it made Jotham feel much better.

"Good morning, small one," Nathan said as Jotham came into the courtyard rubbing his eyes.

"Good morning," Jotham answered with a yawn.

"And what adventures do you have planned for today?" Nathan asked. "It seems that every day brings many surprises since I met you."

Jotham frowned, not understanding the joke. "I want to go to Jerusalem," he said.

Nathan nodded. "Yes, I suspected as much. We shall see what we can arrange. In the meantime," he said, standing, "let us go find a morning meal."

They left the house and walked through the city. Every street was full of color—red and yellow and orange fruit hung from green trees. There were people everywhere, scurrying about, busy with this thing or that thing. The two travelers found the market at the center of town and went to a stall where a man with the longest beard Jotham had ever seen was selling fresh bread. The man was helping another customer.

"I tell you," the merchant was saying, his beard bobbing, "I heard it with my own ears. Decha of Megiddo is dead!"

Jotham sucked in his breath at the words and shot Nathan a look. Nathan shook his head slightly as if to silence Jotham, then they walked away.

"Didn't you hear that!" Jotham whispered when they were alone. "Decha is dead!"

"A rumor, nothing more," Nathan said. "Did you see the body of Decha among the dead last night?"

Jotham shook his head, thinking. "Well, no. But maybe Caleb caught up with him later and killed him!"

"I fear this is not so," Nathan answered.

"But *may*be!" Jotham was quick to add.

He and Nathan quietly moved on, but everywhere they went the talk was the same. Everyone seemed happy at the news. Then they stopped at the booth of a fruit seller.

"How much for these pomegranates?" Nathan asked the vendor.

"Two shekles each!" Nathan scowled at the man, who then laughed. "But on such a holiday as this, one shekel!"

Nathan smiled and brought out his money pouch. "Done!" he said. Then added, "And what makes this such a holiday?"

"Are you the only one in Jericho who does not know?" he asked in astonishment. "Decha of Megiddo is dead!"

"No," Nathan said softly. "I hadn't heard … "

At this Jotham crossed his arms and gave Nathan an "I told you so" smirk.

They filled their stomachs with bread and cheese, and Nathan bought Jotham a new tunic to replace his tattered one. Then he led Jotham out the far side of the city, toward the Jordan River. "I know of a caravan camped there," he said. "I shall try to put you on it."

At this Jotham stopped dead in his tracks and stared at Nathan. Not another caravan, he thought, remembering that was how he came to Decha in the first place.

Nathan looked back at Jotham and smiled. "Fear not, small one," he said, realizing what Jotham was thinking. "The men of this caravan are friends of mine. I met them many years ago when I traveled about. They will care for you as few others could or would."

This helped Jotham relax, and he followed Nathan down toward the Jordan. And there, at the edge of the river, was a sight he had never seen nor would ever forget.

It's easy to hate. All we have to do is find something different about someone and pretend that such a difference makes us superior to them. Or compare our behavior to theirs and think ourselves so much better for not acting the way they do.

In truth, every one of us is the same: we are equally guilty of selfish sin, and we are equally precious in God's sight. Some people may never turn away from their sin, and some people need to be stopped from hurting others. But that doesn't mean that God ever stops loving them, or that we can think ourselves of greater value than they.

The birth we celebrate at Christmas was not given as a gift to the righteous and perfect people of the world. He was a gift to *us*—sinful, self-centered, sometimes self-righteous people. Because we have recognized our sin and done our best to repent of it we have no reason to feel superior. Our repentance should place in us a longing that *all* people could share in the wonderful revelation of Christmas.

Friends

Light two violet candles and the pink candle.

J otham couldn't believe his eyes. He kept staring, expecting the sight to vanish like the mirages he'd seen many times in the desert. But every time he blinked, the image was still there. Camels! Hundreds of them, it seemed. And not the mangy, broken-hooved kind he was used to. These camels were *huge* and *strong* and … and … *young!* They stood proudly, their heads high in the air, gold-braided cords running from the bits in their mouths to the saddles between their humps.

Then there were the people! Two for every one camel, it seemed. All dressed in flowing robes of red and purple and blue. The men all wore turbans of white cloth, and the women had veils over their faces.

The tents of these people were nothing like those of Jotham's father. Instead of goatskin, they were made of a funny cloth that shimmered in the sun and blew easily in the breeze. Each was made of many colors, and came to a point high in the air.

Then, high in the air, Jotham saw the strangest sight of all. A wooden frame covered in colorful cloth danced in the wind. It was held there by a string, and the string led down to the ground where it was held by a small boy. Jotham had never seen anything so magical, and wondered for a moment if evil spirits were at work.

Jotham stood staring at the scene, not believing that any caravan could be so rich or so beautiful. Was he actually going to be traveling with these people, he wondered?

Nathan led Jotham down to the caravan. There he asked around until he finally found the man he was looking for.

"Salamar!" Nathan shouted. The man turned and Jotham saw that he wore a huge turban with a red stone in the center.

"Nathan? *Nathan,* my friend!" The two men met and kissed each other on their cheeks. "Nathan! I am pleased to see you once again. You have grown old, my friend."

Nathan laughed. "I am at least not so young as when we raided the Sultan's armory," he said. Jotham could hardly believe that Nathan knew such a rich man, or that he had ever done something so bold as raid the armory of a sultan! All Jotham ever knew was that Nathan read and copied Scriptures all day.

The two men all but ignored Jotham as they talked about former times. But Jotham didn't mind. He enjoyed watching the people and seeing all the riches this caravan held. Finally Nathan introduced Jotham, and Jotham bowed as he'd been taught. "It is my honor to be in your presence," he said politely.

The older man smiled and bowed. "Perhaps," Salamar said, "I should have my son entertain the boy while we talk."

"That would be excellent," Nathan said, and Jotham nodded his head eagerly. Salamar called to the boy who was holding the string. He was about Jotham's age and, after handing the string to a servant, came running over, his green and black robe flowing behind him.

"Yes, Father," the boy said.

"This is Jotham of Jericho. He is our guest. Treat him as such."

That was all the instruction the boy needed. He bowed deeply to Jotham and said, "May the sheep on a thousand hilltops grace your father's flock, and may you find peace and joy among the tents of my father."

Jotham returned the bow, and then the other boy introduced himself. "I am Ishtar of Persia. It will be my honor to be your host on this most glorious day!"

With the formalities of protocol taken care of, the two boys ran off among the tents and camels,

Ishtar leading the way. Even though they were in Jotham's own land near the town of his birth, Jotham knew it was Ishtar's duty to act as host as long as they were in his father's camp.

As they passed the servant still holding the string, Jotham threw his head back and stared up into the sky. "What *is* that thing," he asked, pointing to the cloth that flew.

Ishtar looked up. "It's a kite," he said plainly. "It flies on the breath of the god of wind."

The two boys wandered through the camp, but Jotham kept looking up at the kite in wonder.

"This is my uncle Jodhpur's tent," Ishtar said, and Jotham gaped at the fine stitchery and colorful designs on the walls of the tent. "He comes from the house of Rajasthan." This meant nothing to Jotham, but he knew it would be impolite to say so. Smaller tents surrounded the large one of Ishtar's uncle. Jotham could see many women inside the tents and asked Ishtar about them. "Those are my uncle's favorite wives," he said. "He left the rest at home."

Jotham was amazed at this. He'd known men who had two or three wives before, but never had he seen dozens of women married to one man. "Where *is* home?" Jotham asked.

"We come from Amaranth. And you are from Jericho, correct?"

"Well, yes, that is where I was born. But my family are shepherds, and we live wherever the grazing is best or there is a market for our sheep and wool."

"Where is your family now?" Ishtar asked. And so Jotham told him. He told him about finding his father's camp deserted—though he didn't say why—and about finding his own grave. He told how he had been picked up by another family of shepherds, how Decha of Megiddo tried to sell him into slavery, and about Nathan's daring rescue in En Gedi. He told of their flight to Qumran, and about Silas being killed here in Jericho, and about Elizabeth and Zechariah and how he, Jotham of Jericho, was going to be the cousin of the Messiah. Then he told of Nathan's second rescue, and how Caleb had killed most of Decha's men.

And when Jotham had finished telling all, Ishtar sat cross-legged in the sand with his head bowed. Jotham sat next to him and after several minutes said, "Ishtar, what is wrong?"

Ishtar spoke slowly, without raising his head. "I hang my head in shame for you, Jotham of Jericho."

Jotham was shocked. "Wh … why?" he asked. "Because many men were killed on my account?"

Ishtar sucked in his breath, then slowly shook his head. "No," he said. "I am embarrassed for you because you have to make up stories to impress me. In my land that is called *poz dadan*, the building of a false image."

Jotham looked at Ishtar, anger rising inside of him like hot lava. "Ishtar," he said through his teeth, "everything I have told you is the truth."

Ishtar just shook his head slowly again and refused to look at Jotham. Finally Jotham pulled him to his feet and said, "Follow me."

Nathan and Salamar were sitting beside a fire drinking tea as Jotham and Ishtar approached. Ishtar's father frowned at the boy and said, "Ishtar! Why do you hang your head in shame?"

Ishtar fidgeted, not wanting to tell on his friend. "Ishtar! Answer!" his father commanded.

Slowly, painfully, Ishtar said, "My friend Jotham has made the *poz dadan*."

Ishtar's father looked from Jotham to Nathan and back. Then to his son said, "What did he tell you?"

Ishtar gave a brief summary, now trying to make it sound less preposterous, in order to keep Jotham's punishment to a minimum. And when he finished, Nathan began laughing, and laughed so hard he fell on his side and knocked over the pitcher of tea. "Ishtar," he said, wiping his eyes, "everything Jotham told you is absolutely true!"

Ishtar's eyes grew as wide as grapefruit. "But this cannot be … " he said, slumping to the ground. "My friend Jotham is no older than myself … to have such adventures!" Ishtar looked at Jotham like he was a holy man, but now it was Jotham who hung his head in shame.

"It is true," he said, "that much has happened to me in the last days. But all of this happened, Ishtar, because I did a bad thing. Nathan's friend Silas lives no more because of my disobedience."

It was quiet for a moment, then Salamar said, "It is a wise man who recognizes the fruits of his errors. It is a *compassionate* man who regrets that fruit. You are truly becoming a man, Jotham of Jericho."

Salamar's kind words felt like a soothing ointment on a burn to Jotham. He smiled a little, then Nathan said, "Jotham, my friend Salamar and his caravan are headed west, toward Jerusalem. He has agreed to take you as far as his course allows."

Jotham's smile doubled in size. This time he was headed home for sure. And with Decha of Megiddo dead, there was *nothing* that could stand in his way!

Sometimes people feel as if they have to make up stories about themselves so people will like them. Sometimes they feel they have to take the real things they do and brag about them. Sometimes people don't feel loved unless they're the center of attention.

But Jesus came to earth exactly for the purpose of letting us know that every one of us is equally loved by God. It does not matter how many people think we're great, and it does not matter how many great things we do.

So, instead of needing other *people* to tell us we're good and acceptable, all we have to do is listen to God's voice whispering in our ear saying, "I love you, just the way you are. It doesn't matter what other people think."

Jotham wasn't bragging when he told Ishtar of his adventures, but Ishtar was right when he said that telling tales and talking about yourself is building a false image. It means that you don't believe you're a very good person, so you have to try to convince others that you are. But there's a simple cure for feelings like that. The cure is only to worry about what *God* thinks of you, rather than what other *people* think of you.

And on the very first Christmas Day, God said to you, "I love you more than anything in this universe!"

Exodus

Light two violet candles and the pink candle.

Only once before in his life had Jotham tasted roast duck. He had loved it then, and he loved it again now. Along with the lamb and the yams and the bread and … well, the feast was like nothing Jotham had ever even *dreamed* of.

They were seated around the inside of Salamar's huge tent, sitting on pillows, legs crossed with forearms resting on their knees. Before each man—and the few boys that were present—sat a small bowl of water. Jotham thought this a strange way to drink water, but he was thirsty so he raised the bowl to his mouth and drank it all down.

Ishtar, sitting next to him, sputtered for a moment, then fell over laughing. "My friend," he said, "this water is not for drinking. It is for washing your hands between courses!"

Jotham's face turned red and several of the men around him laughed. But a girl in pink and white robes with a veil over her face filled his bowl again from a bag of water, and soon everyone except Jotham had forgotten the incident.

The feast was being held in tribute to Nathan, who sat at the place of honor to the right of Salamar. "In celebration of old warriors reunited," he had told the assembly at the beginning of the meal. "And to thank the gods that my friend is safe and well."

"There *is* only one God, you know," Jotham heard Nathan say to Salamar, a mischievous grin on his lips. Salamar had laughed and said, "So there is for you, my brother. And perhaps, so shall there one day be for me!" Jotham could see that it was an old game the two had played, and wondered how Nathan could be friends with someone who believed so differently.

When Jotham was stuffed till he thought roast duck would start coming out his ears, and after the daughters of Salamar had performed a dance, Ishtar led Jotham back to his own little tent, where a place had been made for Jotham.

"I believe I will like having you travel with us," Ishtar said as they lay in the open-end tent watching the stars.

"I believe I will, too," Jotham said. Then a moment later he realized he didn't even know why the caravan was *in* Palestine, or where they were headed.

"We follow the stars," Ishtar said when Jotham asked. "My father and uncles are the Royal Astrologers for His Majesty Sheik Konarak of Amaranth."

Jotham stared at Ishtar in astonishment. *This must be how Ishtar felt when I told him my story,* he thought. Aloud he whispered, "Your father and uncles are *Royalty!?*"

Ishtar laughed. "No, not royalty, but high government officials."

Jotham didn't see much difference. He had never met *any*body important before. "Why are you here?" he asked.

Ishtar lay back with his hands under his head and stared straight up at the stars. "Many months ago my father and uncles saw a sign in the heavens. Ever since then we have traveled west, bringing a message and gifts from the Sultan."

Jotham scrunched up his face. "A message for *whom?*" he asked.

"Why, for your new King, of course," Ishtar answered.

"*What* new King?"

Ishtar sat up and stared as if Jotham had just asked him how to ride a camel. "The new King that is to be born to your people! Surely you know of this great thing!"

Jotham shook his head slowly, feeling like the fool Nathan had once pretended to be. "I … I don't know … " he stammered. Then all of a sudden it struck him.

"The Messiah!" he shouted.

"Messiah?" Ishtar said.

"Yes, the Messiah I told you about. The one whose cousin I will be!"

And together they talked excitedly through the night. Jotham could hardly believe that this huge caravan had been traveling for months just to visit his cousin! Who wasn't even *born* yet!

"How did your father and uncles know about the Messiah?" he asked at one point.

"It is very complicated," Ishtar answered, "and I do not understand it all myself. But I know that two stars arose in a place where they should not have been, and the time of this event somehow told them a new King would be born in this land. So the Sultan sent our caravan to pay his respects and offer gifts of friendship."

Early the next morning, before the sun was up, one of Salamar's servants woke the two boys. "We are leaving," he said. The boys barely had time to get dressed and devour some meat and cheese before all the tents were down and packed onto camels. Jotham gave Nathan a long hug goodbye. "I don't want to leave you," Jotham whispered.

Nathan took his young friend's head in his hands and said, "Jehovah willing, we shall see each other again soon!"

Then, just as the sun rose behind them casting long shadows, Jotham gave one last wave goodbye to Nathan. The caravan molded itself smoothly into a single line heading away from Jericho, and into the hills of Judea.

The route was now becoming familiar to Jotham, but this time he was able to enjoy the trek. *Even if Decha is still alive,* he thought, *he would never dare attack such a mighty caravan as this!* The camels stretched as far ahead of and behind him as he could see. Some carried cargo, some carried women, whom Jotham assumed to be wives of the men, and several carried Ishtar's father and uncles. Every once in a while the men would gather together on their camels and have a discussion, pointing this way and that.

As for the two boys, they walked beside the camel that carried their tent, and which was led by the servant charged with looking after Ishtar. Jotham looked at all the women in the caravan and said, "Ishtar, is your mother among the wives of your father?"

Ishtar looked sad. "My mother is not among the living," he said. "She died when I was very young. She was my father's first wife, and he has never taken another."

Jotham wanted to ask why, but didn't want to seem impolite.

All day the caravan trudged on through the sand and rock. They ate their lunch as they walked because, as Jotham well knew, to stop and start this mighty force would take a great deal of time.

Finally the sun began to set, and the camels were tethered to bushes. The tents were raised almost before Jotham could blink, and he was grateful when he could finally sit by a fire and eat some dinner. He noticed that Ishtar's father and uncles didn't eat, but instead stood around with some funny looking tools in their hands looking into the sky.

After dinner, Jotham walked a short distance from the camp and sat at the base of a lone and scrawny olive tree. He looked into the sky and saw once again "his" star, the one he had been watching since his journey began.

"I'm coming, Mother," he said, and then tears of loneliness began to run down his cheeks.

"What's this?" a voice came out of the dark. "A boy sits alone with tears in his eyes? That must mean that Ishtar of Persia is not doing his job!"

Jotham looked over to see Salamar, Ishtar's father, approaching from the camp. "No, no, sir," Jotham exclaimed. "Ishtar has been a *wonderful* host! But I … "

Salamar held up his hand. "Peace, my friend. I was only joking. But what is it that makes Jotham of Jericho sad on this night?"

Jotham turned his eyes back to the sky. "I miss my family," he said.

"Ah, yes, I understand," said Salamar, sitting down. "We often don't appreciate those we love until we are separated from them." Salamar was silent for a moment, and Jotham could see that his thoughts were far away. After a moment he shook his head and said to Jotham, "But soon we shall be in Jerusalem, and perhaps there you will find word of them." Jotham nodded, then Salamar asked, "And what is it that you stare at in the sky?"

He turned and raised his head to look to where Jotham had been staring, then gasped. "Jotham," he said. "That star! How long have you been watching it?"

Puzzled, Jotham said, "Ever since I left my family."

"That is the star for which we have searched," Salamar said excitedly. "We have not seen it for many days. Even tonight, we looked not an hour ago and it was not there." Then he laughed and jumped up saying, "But for Jotham of Jericho it appears!" Salamar was almost jumping for joy, and it reminded Jotham of the many marriage dances he had seen. "Quickly," he shouted, "we must tell the others!"

Soon there was shouting and pointing throughout the entire caravan and orders were given to strike camp. Before Jotham could even find Ishtar, tents which had only just been put up were taken down and packed. "Quickly!" supervisors were shouting. "We leave at once!"

All this scared Jotham and he thought he had done some terrible thing. By the time he found Ishtar he was crying again. "Jotham! What is it? What's happening?" Ishtar yelled over the excitement in the camp.

"I don't know!" Jotham cried. "All I did was look at a star!"

During the time of King Herod, Magi from the east came to Jerusalem and asked, "Where is the one who has been born king of the Jews? We saw his star in the east and have come to worship him" (Mt 2:1).

Who were these Magi? Where did they come from? Why did they come to worship a foreign king? This story doesn't tell us, and these are questions we will not have answered until we get to heaven.

What this story *does* tell us is that God provided ways for *all* people to come to Jesus. His birth, and the *celebration* of his birth, is not just for any one group of people or for any one church. He came to earth for *all* people, and *accepts* all people wherever they are in their own spiritual journey.

Jesus came to earth to teach us to *love*, not hate, those who have different ways from our own. As we do our Christmas shopping, maybe there's a gift you could prepare for Jesus. Maybe you could make a list of all those you're holding grudges against, or dislike because of the way they act, or whom you snub because they're different from you. Then you could give the list to Jesus on Christmas morning and thank him for each individual and promise him not to feel or say bad things against them anymore.

I guarantee you, no gift would please him more.

Saints

Light two violet candles and the pink candle.

Jotham was dreaming he was on one of the great ships that travel the sea. He had seen such ships as his family camped along the Mediterranean, and now saw himself standing on the bow of one, giving orders. But then there was a foul smell in the air, and his nose tickled. He awoke with a start and discovered his face was buried deep in the fur of a camel's back.

"Yech!" he cried.

"Good morning." Jotham looked around the head of the camel to see where the voice had come from. It was Ishtar's servant, down below, leading the camel. It was only then that he noticed Ishtar riding behind him between the camel's humps.

"Good morning," Jotham called down to the servant. "How did I get up here?"

"Late in the night you fell asleep as you walked, so I lifted you and Ishtar to the camel's back." Suddenly Jotham remembered the excitement of the night before and their quick departure. He had never heard of a caravan traveling at night, but no one seemed to mind the sudden exodus or a lost night of sleep.

Now the morning sun shone on their backs and they were still moving, headed west toward Jerusalem.

"What's going on here!" The voice sounded like the bawl of a newborn lamb. It was Ishtar, now sitting up straight behind Jotham.

"Good morning, friend," Jotham said. "It is morning and we still travel toward Jerusalem."

Jotham saw out of the corner of his eye that Ishtar was looking upward. "The star is gone," he said. "I will speak with my father."

With that Ishtar slid down off the camel and ran forward along the caravan, which wound slowly back and forth in the sun. Jotham decided he'd just as soon stay put and enjoy the ride for a while. A few minutes later Ishtar returned.

"My father said we followed the star all night," Ishtar reported as he walked alongside the camel. "They set their sights on it and follow its course still."

"Will we be stopping today?" Jotham asked.

"Yes, but only for a few hours rest. My father wants to continue on as long as the star appears each night."

"Does he know where we are going?"

"The star takes us in the direction of the great city of Jerusalem, but there is no way to know how far that direction we must go, or if the star will lead us in a different direction."

Jotham nodded, pleased. *Jerusalem is exactly where I want to go,* he thought. *It's where my family will be gathered for the census.*

The caravan continued moving for another hour, then finally a halt was called and everyone lay down for a few hours of sleep. Only a few tents were put up for the women. All the men slept out in the open. Jotham and Ishtar weren't tired, though, since they'd slept on the camel all night. So they set about exploring the desert plateau on which they were camped.

There wasn't much to see on the plateau, mostly scrub brush and sand, but the boys found plenty to do. They chased scorpions and snakes—except for the ones they knew to be dangerous—and tried to catch the few small animals that they saw. But then, just before noon, they saw a rare sight. A silver fox was prowling around the bushes, stalking a hare a few feet away. Carefully, Jotham and Ishtar worked their way through the brush, trying to sneak up on the fox. When they were twenty feet away, the fox heard them and took off running.

The two boys went after it, leaping over scrub brush and rocks, laughing all the way. They scrambled up some boulders at the top of a hill, and Ishtar was about to jump down the other side when Jotham suddenly screamed and grabbed him by the collar.

"Decha!" Jotham screamed. Because there, camped among the rocks, was Decha of Megiddo, looking tired and dirty and beat up and very, very angry.

Ishtar screamed then too, even though he didn't know why. But Jotham knew, and in that instant he saw that they had taken Decha by surprise as he ate his breakfast. Farther down the hill Jotham saw two of Decha's men sleeping on a rock. They had awakened at the screams from the boys and were just getting to their feet.

"Run!" Jotham yelled, and the two boys raced off down the hill. They ran back toward the caravan, but it was in a valley around several hills. Jotham's feet pounded into the ground, sometimes slipping on loose rocks or catching in a bit of sagebrush. Jotham looked behind them and saw that Decha was indeed chasing them, and seemed to be getting closer.

The two boys rounded a hill, and Jotham lost sight of Decha. In the next instant Ishtar screamed. When Jotham looked back Ishtar had disappeared! He skidded to a stop and looked frantically around. Finally he heard a faint cry and, when he looked at where it had come from, he saw a hole in the ground between two clumps of sagebrush. The hole wasn't much bigger than Jotham, and he could understand how Ishtar had failed to see it. A moment later Ishtar's head popped up out of the hole.

"Yech!" he yelled, looking at his dirty tunic in disgust.

Jotham heard the pounding of Decha's footsteps coming from the other side of the hill. In an instant he realized they could never beat Decha back to the caravan now, and they did the only thing there was to do. With a mighty leap he jumped into the hole on top of Ishtar. The two boys slammed into the floor of the cave with a thud. Ishtar started to open his mouth in protest but Jotham quickly clamped his hand over his friend's face. Both boys listened as Decha's running feet passed the cave and kept going. After a few moments, Jotham let go of Ishtar.

"Ow!" yelled the Persian boy. "That *hurt!*"

"Trust me," Jotham said, panting, "it would hurt a great deal more if Decha were to catch us."

Jotham's eyes began to adjust to the light, and he could see that the cave was actually part of a tunnel that ran for a great distance both directions into the dark. He thought for a moment, then tore a piece off his tunic and wrapped it around a stick. As he had seen Nathan do, he then found a flint stone and lit his makeshift torch.

"What are you doing?" Ishtar asked.

"We're going to follow this tunnel," Jotham answered.

"We're *what!*"

"We cannot go back outside," Jotham continued. "Decha and his men have probably already figured out we did not make it back to the caravan and are hiding somewhere. They will be searching the area above us."

Ishtar looked at the rock ceiling over their heads and shuddered. "Then let us move quickly," he said. "Which direction shall we go?"

Jotham looked back and forth, then turned to his left. "This way," he said, and slowly they climbed through the jagged edges of the tunnel with Jotham in the lead. All of a sudden the floor of the tunnel leveled out. Men have been here before, Jotham thought to himself. The floor is too flat and smooth to be just a cave.

The boys edged their way forward, hearts pounding in their chests, thinking that maybe this wasn't such a good idea. Jotham kept imagining scorpions hiding in the dark cracks of the rocks, and snakes hanging from the ceiling. He was just about to say they should turn back when Decha's voice came haunting them through the cave.

"Little one," came the faint but evil voice. "Little one! Come back to me! I am going to kill you, little one! You may run, but I am going to catch you and kill you!"

Jotham's heart raced and he pushed on through the darkness, not caring anymore about snakes or scorpions.

"Friend of the little one," came the voice again. "Listen to me! I will not harm you! Bring your friend to me and I shall spare your life!"

Jotham's eyes grew wide and he looked at Ishtar. Ishtar gave him a look that said, "Yeah, like I'd really do that!" Jotham smiled, then they ran on. They barely even noticed as they passed through an archway cut into the rock, but a moment later they skidded to a stop and screamed once again.

"It is death!" Ishtar cried.

"Run!" Jotham shouted.

But both boys just stood there, heaving great, terrified breaths, transfixed by what they saw. Cut into the walls of the cave in front of them were small alcoves. And in each alcove was a dead body wrapped in cloth.

"We must leave this place," Ishtar cried. But neither of them could move. They inched their way forward, looking at the bodies in the torch light. The alcoves were cut out of the rock and extended as far as the boys could see. Each was slightly bigger than the corpse it held, and each body was wrapped in fine linen cloth.

"Who would do such a terrible thing?" Ishtar asked, his nose scrunched in disgust.

"*What* terrible thing?" Jotham panted, his own face twisted in horror at the sight.

"To put dead bodies in a cave with no sarcophagus?"

"What's a sacrifagust?"

"Sarcophagus," Ishtar corrected. "The burial box of the dead."

"I've never *seen* anyone buried in a box before. My people just wrap dead ones in burial cloths, and cover them with spices."

Ishtar thought this was pretty crude and very cruel, but didn't say anything more. The boys realized that Decha could reach them at any moment, and started up the tunnel again. After a few minutes, the evil voice returned, a little louder this time.

"Little one, look!" it said. "It is the bodies of your ancestors! What a good place for you to die!" Then there came a screeching, evil laugh and Jotham ran just a little faster.

Jotham and Ishtar ran for what seemed like hours. They were almost as afraid of the dead bodies as they were of the evil voice that slithered through the dark every few minutes. Finally the tunnel ended in a huge room filled with stone carvings. Jotham's torch was getting short now, and he tore another length from his tunic.

The room seemed as big as a temple to the boys, and all around its walls were cut tall archways that led to other tunnels. The archways were decorated with carved images of ancient ancestors in long robes. One was of Moses parting the sea. Another showed a man being spit out by a great fish. In others men and women were leading camels, fighting wars, praising God.

Then, in the dimming light, they came across a flat, white stone with writing on it, and Ishtar gasped. Jotham looked at him in amazement. "You can *read* this," he said, surprised that any boy of ten could read such writing.

"Yes," Ishtar said, barely able to whisper. "It says, 'We wait in peace, for this is the place where the Messiah shall come to earth!'"

At that moment the voice of the devil cut through the dark only inches behind Jotham's ear. "I am here, little one," Decha hissed like a snake.

And then Jotham screamed for the last time.

"A day of the Lord is coming.… On that day his feet will stand on the Mount of Olives, east of Jerusalem, and the Mount of Olives will be split in two … " (Zec 14:1, 4).

Many Jews are so anxious for the coming of the Messiah that they have themselves buried near the place where they believe he will make his appearance—on the Mount of Olives near Jerusalem. While we Christians believe that the Messiah has *already* arrived, it is true that the Bible tells of his *second* coming to that mountain.

What we believe should make a difference in the way we live. Advent is the perfect time to take a deep look at our spiritual lives. Does our religion make a difference in the way we think and act toward others? Do we love the Lord enough to let him take our self-centeredness away?

"Search me, O God, and know my heart; test me and know my anxious thoughts. See if there is any offensive way in me, and lead me in the way everlasting" (Ps 139:23-24).

Christmas will be that much merrier if we can say that verse with sincerity, and allow God to shed his light on the dark tunnels of our souls.

Simeon

Light two violet candles and the pink candle.

Jotham spun around in terror. In the orange light of the torch he saw Decha's face only inches away. It looked like the face of a mad jackal, and this sent more stabs of fear through Jotham's heart.

"Yes, I am here, little one," Decha hissed again. "And now you are finally mine!"

Decha grabbed the front of Jotham's tunic, and Jotham could smell the foul stench of Decha's breath. Jotham plunged his torch square into Decha's face. Decha screamed and let go of Jotham, holding his face in his hands.

"Run!" Jotham commanded Ishtar, and the two boys took off down one of the side tunnels. Behind them they could hear Decha cursing and yelling more threats.

The boys ran as fast as a camel in a race, the torch barely lighting the path ahead. A moment later the tunnel turned, but the boys didn't, and they crashed head-first into a skeleton hanging in an alcove. They both fell to the ground, the bones of some long-dead ancestor crashing down around them like a cage.

Ishtar screamed and began thrashing about like a fish out of water. Jotham, too, felt a scream climbing up his throat. But all of a sudden the anger inside him squashed the scream. Furious now, he threw aside the bones and stood to his feet. "That's *it!*" he yelled. "I can't take this anymore!"

With that, he picked up the torch and started back up the tunnel, toward Decha.

"Where are you going?" Ishtar cried in panic.

"I'm going to kill Decha!"

"You're *what!?*"

Jotham stopped and turned back toward his friend. "I'm going to kill Decha. I'm sick and tired of running away!" Then he picked up a bone from the skeleton and threw it as hard as he could up the tunnel as he yelled, "I'm not scared of jackals anymore!"

As those words echoed down the rock walls, Jotham stomped off once more, headed back toward Decha.

He found him a short ways up the tunnel.

"Well, little one," Decha smiled, his face black and red with burns. "I'm glad you have come to your senses. It was wise of you to return to me. I will make your death less painful." Decha bounced his fingers off each other as he thought about this for a moment, then added, "Well, perhaps not." He laughed his low and evil laugh, and in that moment Jotham rushed at him with the torch.

Decha was ready this time, though, and stepped aside neatly. Grabbing Jotham by the back of his tunic, Decha spun the boy around and shoved him against the tunnel wall. The torch flew from Jotham's hand, landing on the tunnel floor, making Decha look even more evil with the light coming from below.

Jotham ran at Decha again, but Decha caught him and spun him around, locking Jotham's neck in the crook of his arm. "Who do you think you are to resist me so?" Decha hissed. "Am I not the great Decha of Megiddo? Am I not five times your size? Am I not the most … " And with that, Jotham heard a loud *crack* and felt Decha slump to the floor. Jotham turned and saw Ishtar standing behind Decha, a human leg bone in his hands.

"Well, I couldn't let him hurt my best of all friends!" Ishtar exclaimed. Jotham grinned, but then his face returned to fear. Coming up the tunnel behind Ishtar were two torches, carried by Decha's two henchmen.

"Come, we must find a way out of this place," Jotham said. He picked up the torch, then the two boys headed up the tunnel once more. In a few moments they passed the skeleton they had crashed into, but this time they turned with the walls. They ran as fast as they could in only the dim torchlight, not wanting to smash into another wall. After a few moments they heard Decha roar in anger, and they knew they had only a few minutes before the demons would catch up to them.

That's when they heard the voices.

Faintly at first, very far away. Then just a bit louder, or perhaps closer. In the dark it sounded like wind echoing off the walls. But after listening very closely Jotham eventually decided it was … he thought … the voices of men!

"Ishtar! Listen!" he commanded.

"I *have* been listening," he exclaimed. "Let us go at once!"

The boys turned down another tunnel toward the voices. Jotham didn't know if the voices belonged to good men or bad, but he didn't much care. He'd gladly be sold into slavery rather than smell the breath of Decha again!

Jotham and Ishtar turned another corner and gasped. There was light ahead! They continued on and with each step the light got brighter. Then they rounded one last bend and saw a beautiful sight: an opening in the end of the tunnel, with two men silhouetted against the blue sky outside. The men had their backs to the boys, and were just getting ready to roll a large stone across the entrance to the cave.

"Stop!" Jotham shouted, "Wait!"

The two men jumped three feet into the air and screamed the scream of men frightened to death. Then they turned and ran away from the tunnel, dropping instantly out of sight down a slope. Jotham and Ishtar didn't care about the men, they just wanted out. Running at full speed they headed for the opening to the cave. But just before they got there, a huge man stepped squarely into the center of the opening and blocked their way.

Now it was the boys who screamed the scream of frightened men. They dug their heels in and a shower of dirt flew ahead of them as they slid to a stop. "Who is there!" the voice demanded, low and loud.

Jotham swallowed hard. "It is Jotham of Jericho," he yelled back, "and his friend Ishtar!"

"Are you of the living or of the dead?" the voice asked.

"We are of the living," Jotham answered, "though not for long if you do not allow your servants to leave this awful place!"

"Come then," the voice answered, "or be locked in with the dead!"

Jotham and Ishtar wasted no time scrambling through the opening and out into the fresh air and bright sunshine. Then they turned and began pushing on the stone and yelling at the man. "Hurry, help us!" they yelled. "A devil follows us!"

With the man's help, the two boys rolled the stone across the opening to the cave. At the last possible second Decha's hand shot through the opening and grabbed the stone, trying to push it back. The weight of the stone and the strength of the man were too much, however, and Decha screamed from inside the tunnel as the stone rolled closed, smashing his hand.

Jotham and Ishtar turned and leaned back against the stone, their eyes closed, panting like thirsty dogs. After a few moments Jotham opened his eyes and what he saw sent a lightning bolt through his bones. Because there, on the other side of the valley, sitting atop a hill like the richest crown on the head of any king, sat the city of Jerusalem.

An hour later Jotham and Ishtar were in such different circumstances that they could not even have dreamed it if they had tried. They were sitting at the center of a rich house, at the edge of a pool, their feet dangling in the water, eating coconuts and dates.

"For what do you wait, Simeon?" Jotham asked, slurping some coconut juice. Simeon was much older than the boys had first thought upon seeing his silhouette, and much nicer too. He had just been explaining to them how he helped bury the bodies of the dead saints while he waited.

"I wait," he said, "for the coming of the Messiah." And at that, Jotham smiled.

Once they had convinced Simeon that they were not ghosts, Jotham and Ishtar had quickly explained to him how they had come to be lost in the tunnels. With eyes so kind they reminded Jotham of his grandfather, Simeon had given them some water, then led them here to his own villa where he ordered them fed and bathed. He then sent a rider with a message for Ishtar's father.

"But what do you *mean* that you wait?" Jotham asked again.

Simeon stood, his hands behind his back, and walked slowly to a window overlooking Jerusalem below. "I was standing in this very place several years ago," he said. "I had just returned from burying my wife, and was about to go to the temple to offer a sacrifice for my sins. I was, I'm afraid, being rather selfish at that moment, thinking that with my wife dead I really had no reason to live. It was at that moment," Simeon continued, his voice now growing soft, "that I felt the presence of Jehovah upon me. I fell face down on the floor, right here," and he tapped his foot to indicate the exact place. "And I heard a voice speak to me just as we speak now."

"What did the voice say?" Jotham gasped.

"The voice, the Holy Spirit of Jehovah himself, said to me, 'Fear not, Simeon of Nazareth, for you shall surely not die until the day of Israel's consolation!"

Jotham was quiet for a few moments, then asked, "Does that mean the coming of the Messiah?"

Simeon nodded. "Yes, it does."

Jotham pulled his feet out of the water and walked over to stand next to Simeon. He looked out the window toward Jerusalem, its temple reaching to the sky like a gold and ruby mountain, and its high stone wall surrounding it like a belt. Then he looked to the left, to the other side of the valley and the thousands of graves on the hill. Simeon had called it the Mount of Olives. He said it was where tradition held that the Messiah would return to reclaim the souls of the saints.

Then Jotham turned to Simeon, feeling both grateful for his hospitality and a closeness as if they shared a common experience. "Simeon," he said softly. "I think perhaps I should tell you a secret."

Now there was a man in Jerusalem called Simeon, who was righteous and devout. He was waiting for the consolation of Israel, and the Holy Spirit was upon him … When the parents brought in the child Jesus to do for him what the custom of the Law required, Simeon took him in his arms and praised God, saying: "Sovereign Lord,… now dismiss your servant in peace. For my eyes have seen your salvation,… and for glory to your people Israel" (Lk 2:25ff).

Simeon waited patiently.

Can *you?*

Simeon recognized the Messiah when he saw him.

Would *you?*

Simeon embraced the Messiah with all his heart.

Do *you?*

Simeon was satisfied to have only Jesus.

Are *you?*

Searching

Light two violet candles and the pink candle.

"My friend," the man in the dirty tunic said, "can I interest you in a bit of baklava?" Jotham looked at Ishtar, who then looked at the pastry the man held out. Ishtar gave a slight shake of the head, then Jotham said, "No, thank you." They pushed on through the crowd, trying to look into every crack and alley for a sign of Jotham's father.

"You are missing a rare delicacy!" the man in the dirty tunic yelled after them. The two boys ignored him, knowing the unwritten rules of haggling did not require them to respond.

Jerusalem was so big! Jotham couldn't imagine why all these people would want to live together, shoulder to shoulder, crammed in like … well, like a flock of sheep. The air was foul with the stench of manure and sweat, and red-faced men pulled camels, goats, and donkeys through the narrow, winding streets.

But for all of that, Jotham found Jerusalem fascinating. You could buy just about anything you could ever want, he decided—if you had the money, of course. And there were more kinds of people moving about than Jotham ever knew existed: white-faced, black-faced, red-faced; women with veils and women with funny feathered hats. But the thing that sent a tingle through Jotham's chest every time he saw it was the soaring tower of the temple that overshadowed the entire city. Everywhere they went—in the market, up an alley, or behind the stables—Jotham could always look up and see at least a part of the temple spires overhead.

"Is that him?" Ishtar said, pointing to a middle-aged man with a beard. Jotham's heart skipped a beat as he searched out the face Ishtar pointed to, then sighed as he said, "No. But he is a very close likeness."

They continued searching, Jotham driven by hope and Ishtar driven by a desire to see his friend happy again. Ishtar could only guess what Jotham's family looked like. But still, two sets of eyes are better than one.

"What is *baklava?*" Jotham asked.

"It is a sweet and flaky pastry that is full of honey and nuts. It is the best of my people."

"So why didn't we get some?"

"Because the baklava the man offered was camel dung compared to *real* baklava. Besides," he said, "we have no money."

Jotham shrugged and went back to inspecting the faces in the crowd. Simeon, he knew, was searching another part of the city. With only a description of Jotham's family it would be difficult, but Jotham was confident that if his family was to be found, Simeon could find them.

The two boys had enjoyed their time with Simeon. When Jotham had told him of his many adventures, and about all he had learned of the coming of the Messiah, Simeon got so excited the boys were afraid the angel of death would come to him early. But he had finally calmed down, and they had talked late into the night about the Messiah. Jotham made Simeon tell the story of the Holy Spirit's visit over and over, and Simeon kept saying, "And you are *sure* that Ishtar's father followed a rising star?" Then a few moments later he'd say, "Are you *sure* that Nathan said the time is close?" Jotham would nod his head rapidly each time and say, "Yes, yes, I'm sure!"

"Ishtar, look!"

Ishtar raised his head to look where Jotham was pointing. Over the top of the city wall they could see a huge caravan descending from the wilderness of Judea to the Kidron Valley, which separated it from Jerusalem. "It is my father," Ishtar yelled. Together the boys ran out the Lion's Gate in the city wall and met up with the caravan just as it reached the bottom of the valley.

"Father!" Ishtar cried when he saw him. The two hugged for a long time, then Ishtar had much explaining to do. It made Jotham feel even more sad that he could not find his own father in all of Jerusalem.

"When the servant of Simeon rode to our camp and told me you were alive, it was as if you were born again!" Salamar said. He told how the entire caravan, even the women, had searched every rock and bush in the desert, and how he had sent for Nathan to help them search. Then he looked up to the Mount of Olives and marvelled that the boys had come so far through the tunnels.

Just then Simeon walked up and Jotham introduced him to Salamar. "I am in your debt, for caring for my son. May your God favor you richly for your kindness."

Simeon reported finding no trace of Jotham's family. Then Salamar said, "Jotham, you are welcome to stay with our caravan if you would like. We will camp here tonight. My brothers and I have decided to speak with your king. Surely *he* will know where the babe is to be born."

Jotham was amazed that Ishtar's father was actually going to visit King Herod! He had never before known anyone who could just walk in and see the king.

Simeon, who was now responsible for Jotham, said Jotham could stay with the caravan or at his own home, whichever Jotham desired. Then Jotham asked if Ishtar could help him search the city some more. "No, that will not be possible," Salamar said. "His place is at my side as I visit your king."

Jotham thanked everyone and said he would stay with the caravan that night, and then with Simeon after it left. He walked with Ishtar and his father and uncles as far as the Lion's Gate, then set out on his own to search. The only place he hadn't looked, he decided finally, was in the temple itself. He had never been to the temple and wasn't sure how to act if he went there, but five minutes later found himself climbing the white marble stairs that led up a short hill to the temple mount.

Once on top, Jotham's eyes grew wide. Surely this is heaven, he thought! Before him was a courtyard big enough to hold ten flocks of sheep, made entirely of white and blue marble that reflected the bright sunlight into Jotham's eyes. Around the entire court stood rows and rows of white columns, a narrow beam connecting them all together like some unfinished roof. To the right, between the columns, Jotham could see the Mount of Olives on the other side of the Kidron Valley. The whole hillside was tiled with white grave markers and tombs. Far below in the green of the valley, Ishtar's caravan camped along the creek.

Then Jotham looked between the columns to his left and saw all of Jerusalem spread out below. The city wall, as high as five camels, cut a jagged course around the city. Narrow streets wound around the buildings of clay and stone, and Jotham could now see the market where the man had offered them baklava. On the other side of the city, against the opposite wall, he saw three towers and the palace of Herod.

Jotham stood for a long time trying to take in every detail of this great city. Then he turned his attention to the temple in front of him. White stone rose out of the marble to tower over his head. Four great columns stood guard over the entrance to the temple itself. It seemed that everything he saw was decorated with designs of gold reminding him of flowers and seashells. Another short wall separated Jotham from the temple. He asked a man if he could go inside. The man looked at Jotham, dressed now in a blue tunic given him by Simeon, and said, "Of course. But you must stay in the Court of Women." The man didn't need to tell Jotham this was because he had not yet reached the age of thirteen.

Jotham walked up another set of marble stairs and through a small gate in the wall. He came out the other side of the gate and looked up to see the temple reaching for the sun over his head. It seemed to be higher than the clouds, and Jotham wondered how mortal men had ever built such a thing.

He was in the Court of Women now, and knew he could not pass through the gate in the final wall that protected the temple. At least not until he was thirteen. But even here there were hundreds of women and children, and even some men, bringing sacrifices or praying or just standing around talking. Along one side of the wall were wooden tables set up with weights and measures. Men at the tables sold lambs and birds and grain for sacrifices. It seemed sort of strange, Jotham thought, to see men selling things in such a holy place.

Jotham wandered among the people looking for any sign of his mother or sisters. A woman so old that Jotham thought she should surely be dead sat against a column praying. Every once in a while she would shout something, and the people around her would laugh, and one woman even spat on her.

For what little was left of the afternoon, Jotham continued searching through the Court of Women. When he had gone around the entire temple, he decided to go back to the caravan. He was headed toward the gate leading out of the Court of Women when he felt a tug on his tunic. He looked down to see the crazy old woman the others had been making fun of, pulling on his clothes.

"Boy!" she croaked, her ancient lips barely able to form the words. "The Messiah is coming!"

This was no surprise to Jotham and he said simply, "Yes, I know."

The look of shock on the old woman's face—which was so thin that she already looked dead—made Jotham think he had killed her for good! She looked at him for a long time, as if she could see inside his head and know what he was thinking. Then she got a strange and distant look on her face. She pulled him close until his face was only inches from her own. "I am Anna, daughter of Phanuel," she said softly, and Jotham wondered if that should mean something to him. "And I tell you, that the one you seek you will find in Bethlehem!"

We each spend our lives searching, and we are all searching for the same thing, though we do it in many different ways. We will go to extreme lengths to try to find what we're looking for, and many times we hurt others as we search.

The thing we search for is not a person or an animal, or even a god necessarily. The thing we search for is the most important thing in all our lives. Without it we don't care to live. In fact, when people think they haven't found it, they often become depressed or suicidal.

Without this thing there is a hole in our chest the size of a watermelon. It makes us act in selfish ways, treat others unkindly, and always want our own way. We try to fill this hole with popularity, power, or self-praise; but nothing is ever good enough to take away the pain of that empty space. What is this thing that each of us searches for to the exclusion of all else? It is simply the knowledge that somebody loves us. The knowledge, the belief, that someone, somewhere, thinks we're important.

The truth is, that no matter who we are or what we've done, there is One who loves us more than anyone else ever could or would. "Jesus loves me, this I know, for the Bible tells me so." The problem is, most of us don't really believe that. We think we need *people* to love us in order to be of any value.

So sometimes if we do something we think is great, but nobody compliments us, we feel badly. Or if someone else seems to be the center of attention, we get angry. Or if our friends pay attention to someone else, we get jealous.

Yes, each of us is searching for exactly the same thing—someone to tell us we're pretty or handsome enough, someone to tell us we're good enough, someone to tell us we are loved. But the secret of Christmas is simply this: you will find the One you search for in Bethlehem!

Special Instructions for Week Four

Because Advent always starts on Sunday, but Christmas is on a different day each year, Advent can last anywhere from twenty-one to twenty-eight days. Therefore the last week of *Jotham's Journey* is in seven parts. The following table will help you determine which parts to read each day this week, depending on which day Christmas *Eve* falls. (See the chart on page 168.)

Instead of devotional thoughts, each part is followed by a question to consider. Use the question or questions of the day as a discussion starter, or consider them seriously in your own heart. But either way, have a wonderful week: Christmas is coming!

If Christmas Eve is on:

Read these parts on:		Sun	Mon	Tues	Wed	Thur	Fri	Sat
	Sunday	1-7	1-5	1-3	1-2	1-2	1	1
	Monday		6-7	4-5	3-4	3	2	2
	Tuesday			6-7	5	4	3	3
	Wednesday				6-7	5	4	4
	Thursday					6-7	5	5
	Friday						6-7	6
	Saturday							7

Jotham's Journey

Part One

Light the violet candles and the pink candle each day.

"No, no, I cannot allow it!"

"But, *Simeon*," Jotham cried, "she *told* me I'd find my family in *Bethlehem!*"

Simeon shook his head once again. "I'm sorry, Jotham, but I cannot allow you to run off to Bethlehem just because some crazy old woman stares you in the eye!"

"Well fine then!" Jotham shouted, "I'll just run … " He stopped suddenly and got a pained look on his face. He had been about to say he would just run away, but then remembered that was how this whole nightmare had started. And why Silas was dead.

He lowered his head and his voice and said, "Very well, I will obey."

Simeon smiled the kind of smile that can only come with age and wisdom. "I know it is difficult, Jotham," he said, rubbing the back of the boy's head. "But you must understand that Abigail has had a difficult life. She sits in the temple and says whatever pops into her mind to anyone passing by. Why, one time," he said, sitting on the bench next to Jotham, "she told me that a flock of pigs were going to fly to my house to sit in honor at a banquet."

Jotham didn't smile. He hardly heard Simeon. Something was wrong here, and he was searching every corner of his brain to figure out what.

Simeon was smiling, though, and now added, "They never did come here, you know."

One part of Jotham's mind was wondering what Simeon was talking about, while another continued to search for the mistake he knew was hanging in the air. Finally he found what he was looking for. "I think I got her name wrong," he said slowly. "Her name wasn't Abigail. It was … Amon. No ,no, that's a boy's name. Anna! Her name was Anna!"

Now *Simeon* stopped smiling and his face turned pale. "Did she tell you her *full* name?" he asked.

"I think so," Jotham said, trying to remember. His forehead wrinkled into a frown as he forced his brain to think. "It was something like, Panua, or Pharoa … "

"Could it have been 'Phanuel?'" Simeon whispered.

"Yes! That was it."

Simeon was silent for a long moment, then finally whispered, "Jotham, you must go to Bethlehem at once!"

People were pushing and shoving like cattle in a stampede. Jotham had never seen this many people on a road before. He was used to being alone in the wide open meadows where his flock grazed. Now it seemed as if the whole world were going to Bethlehem.

"Why don't all these people just go home!" Jotham yelled to Simeon over the noise of the crowd. Simeon chuckled.

"That's exactly what they're doing, Jotham." Then he explained. "These people are all returning to the city of their birth for the census."

As soon as Simeon had found out it was Anna of Phanuel who had pointed Jotham toward the City of David, he knew he must take him there. Anna was a devout woman who was close to God. She fasted and prayed all day and almost never left the temple. Like Simeon, Anna was waiting for the arrival of the Messiah. She, too, was full of the Holy Spirit.

So here they were now, on a narrow, winding road that led them through the six miles from Jerusalem to Bethlehem. Simeon had laughed at Jotham's impatience, but as a donkey stepped on *his* big toe he began to think that maybe the whole world *was* on this road!

"Is that it?" Jotham yelled for the twelfth time, having seen a small building up ahead.

"No, that is not it either," Simeon said patiently. What was taking so long, Jotham wondered. It felt like *days* since they had said goodbye to Ishtar and left Simeon's house.

Jotham went back to searching the hillsides. All along the route there were shepherds tending their flocks on the hills overlooking the road. But none were the sheep of his father, and he saw no one he recognized.

Then they crested a hill, and Jotham saw a small group of buildings below. "*That* is Bethlehem," Simeon said with a smile in his voice.

Consider: If you were Jotham, do you think you might be as eager as he is to get to Bethlehem and find your family? Do you think Jotham might even find something better there? We are anxious to get to Christmas, but do you think there might be a better reason than just gifts under the tree?

Part Two

Jotham was disappointed. It was so small! Not a tenth the size of Jerusalem. There were about as many buildings in the whole town as lambs in Jotham's flock.

As they reached the edge of Bethlehem, many of the people on the road went straight through on their way to other places. But many stopped. They were looking for lodging and food. "Do you know where Hasrah lives?" Simeon asked, but Jotham shook his head. Simeon stopped where a man was sitting on a wooden bench grinding an axe. "Excuse me, sir," Jotham said. "Could you point me to the Inn of Hasrah?"

"Two houses that way," the man pointed with his axe toward the road they had been traveling. "Go right and then three buildings over."

"Thank you," Simeon said, and handed him a small coin. Simeon took Jotham by the hand once more and led him through the crowd. Hasrah's inn was two stories high and made of stone, and it was right where the man had said. As they opened the huge wooden door and walked in, Hasrah grinned like a bridegroom.

"Jotham of Jericho!" he yelled. "By all that is good and holy I thought I'd never see you again!"

Jotham gave Hasrah a big hug. "It is good to see you," he said. "And I bring you glad tidings!"

"Oh, and what is that?"

Jotham stepped back and grinned. "Nathan of Qumran is alive!"

Hasrah almost fell over, but grabbed for the table. Then he sat down. "That *is* good news," he said. "But how do you *know* this?" Jotham explained all about being kidnapped by Decha and the rescue by Nathan and Caleb. "But our friend Silas?" he asked when Jotham was finished.

"Silas really *was* killed by Decha," Jotham said softly.

Hasrah hung his head in sadness. "May he live and reign with Jehovah," he said. A moment later he raised his head and smiled. "At least Nathan is alive, and I shall have to reward my friend Seth the next time I'm in Jericho. But now, my young shepherd, I must return to work. As you can see, I have much of it!"

Jotham looked around the tiny inn. People and belongings were stacked *everywhere*, even on the narrow wooden stairs that led to the upper room, and it seemed as if not another person could cram into this place. Simeon asked Hasrah if he would take charge of Jotham, to which Hasrah agreed saying, "I could certainly use an extra pair of hands!"

"May you find your family safe and well," Simeon said to Jotham with a bow. Jotham gave Simeon a hug, and decided he was tired of making wonderful new friends only to have to say goodbye to them right away.

"I will tell my father of your kindness," he said. Simeon bowed also to Hasrah and thanked him, then he was off to Jerusalem.

"Well, Jotham," Hasrah said, wrapping his arm around Jotham's shoulders, "perhaps you could start by cleaning out the stable."

Consider: Jotham had great expectations of what Bethlehem would be like, but was disappointed at the tiny village he found. He did not understand that great things can come in unexpected ways. What expectations do you have for Christmas? Do you suppose there is something about Christmas that is great enough to make it a special day, even if you don't get any presents?

Part Three

For the next two hours Jotham found himself in the stable under the inn, raking out the old hay and manure and replacing it with clean hay. This wasn't why he had come to Bethlehem, but he was grateful that Hasrah had taken him in, and he would show his appreciation in any way he could.

It was warm in the stable, the heat from the animals was held in by thick stone walls. There were two sheep, a goat, and four donkeys which belonged to some of the travelers. One of the donkeys had a patch of white hair on his forehead that Jotham thought made the animal look just like his grandfather. He even started calling him "Father."

The animals were messing up the new hay just about as fast as Jotham could pitch it, and he felt as if he'd been working in this smelly stable his whole life. Soon his arms were so sore he could no longer toss the piles of hay, so he sat on the edge of the wooden feeding trough to rest. The donkey he called "Father" came over and nuzzled his hand.

"Hello, Father," Jotham said. "Would you like a treat?" The donkey rubbed its head against Jotham's arm, so Jotham reached into the manger and pulled out a handful of hay. Father ate the clover and alfalfa straight from Jotham's hand, and Jotham giggled at the way the animal's lips tickled his palm.

The manger Jotham sat on was a rectangular box about the size of his sleeping mat and as high as his waist. Rough planks of olive wood formed the sides, and were gnarled along the top edges where dozens of animals had sharpened their teeth. When Father had finished his snack, Jotham rested his hand on the edge of the trough, then pulled it back sharply with an "Ouch!" A sliver from one of the chew marks had stuck in his hand, and it took several minutes and a few tears before he extracted the bit of wood.

Finally Jotham put some fresh hay in the feeding trough, washed his hands, and then reported back to Hasrah. "I have finished cleaning the stable," he said.

Hasrah smiled. "And did you put new hay in the manger?" When Jotham nodded Hasrah said,

"Well then, I have another important job for you." Jotham felt his insides get disappointed again, but tried not to let it show. He would do whatever anyone asked of him from now on, he had decided, even if it meant putting aside what *he* wanted to do. "I need you," Hasrah was saying, "to go search for your family!"

Jotham got a huge grin on his face. "I would go and help you myself," Hasrah continued, then with a sweep of his hand around the crowded room added, "but as you see, I have my hands full."

"That's fine," Jotham said. "I'm just grateful for the chance to look myself."

Jotham headed out the door and Hasrah called after him, "Be back by the time the sun sets, Jotham of Jericho," and Jotham waved back.

Consider: Jotham was in a place where a wondrous event was about to take place, but he didn't even know it. Many people today spend an entire Christmas season without ever realizing how close they are to its true wonder. How can you prevent Christmas from being just another holiday?

Part Four

As small as Bethlehem was, it seemed *huge* with all the people and animals that crowded the streets. Just like in Jerusalem, Jotham searched each face to see if it belonged to his father or brother or mother. "The one you seek you will find in Bethlehem," Anna had said. So far, all he had found were a lot of people pushing and shoving, trying to buy lamp oil or sell their animals to pay taxes. Some were just looking for a place to spend the night.

In the middle of the town was a place where the two biggest roads crossed. It was here, right in the middle of the crossing, that three men sat at a long wooden table. Jotham could tell these men were Jewish by the red and blue pattern of their shawls. Each was hunched over a stack of parchments and each was busy writing with a quill. Next to each man was a large cloth and leather bag.

Behind the table where the three men sat stood another man with skin so white that Jotham thought he must have bathed himself in goat's milk. He wore a white tunic with a light-blue robe over the top and stood with his arms folded, watching everything that happened at the table carefully. Surrounding all four men and the table was a ring of Roman soldiers wearing helmets, swords, and bright red capes with gold stitching along the edge. The ring of soldiers took up almost the whole intersection, forcing travelers on the two roads to crowd their way around them next to the buildings.

Stretching out from the soldiers and down one street as far as Jotham could see were three lines of dusty, sweaty, tired-looking men. Some held bundles in their arms, others talked in groups of three or four, still others clutched small leather bags so tightly to their chests that Jotham thought they must surely contain great treasure.

Every few minutes a man at the front of a line would step through the soldiers and approach the wooden table. Peeking between two soldiers whose capes were blowing in the wind, Jotham could see the men who were standing and talking with those at the table. Then each of the standing men would open a purse or a bundle and extract several coins. These they gave to the collectors. This went on and on.

Occasionally the milk-white man would point to one of the standing men and say something. A guard would then go with that man and return a few minutes later, nodding his head at the milk-white man. Then everything would proceed as normal. But once after the guard had dragged a man away in chains, he returned with him still in chains. He threw him on the ground in front of the table. Everything stopped as the authority talked to the soldier. He turned and made a loud announcement to everyone who could hear his high-pitched voice.

"This man has tried to cheat Caesar!" he yelled. "He thought he could deceive Rome by not declaring a newborn son! Let all men present witness the fruit of his lies!"

At that the biggest, most powerful soldier—who must be the leader of the other soldiers, Jotham decided—stepped to the center of the ring and pulled a long, coiled whip from his belt. Jotham had never seen a whipping before, and his stomach felt as if it was full of snakes each time the whip sliced through the air and onto the back of the man on the ground. Finally, when it seemed as if the man must surely be dead, two soldiers forced him to his feet and dragged him away.

So this is a census, Jotham thought.

For more than an hour Jotham watched, fascinated by the amount of money that was handed over and deposited in the cloth and leather bags. Slowly he began to realize that his father, too, would have to stand in this line and pay his taxes. And then, like a flash of lightning that lights up the whole world, Jotham realized that his father might have already been here. And if he had, then his name would be on one of those parchment lists!

"Excuse me, sir," Jotham said, tugging on the red cape of one of the soldiers. The soldier's arms were folded and his face was outlined by his metal helmet. He looked down at Jotham.

The soldier snorted a laugh through his nose. "Get away from here, Jew," he said, shoving Jotham back so hard he fell on his bottom in the dust of the road. "The business of Rome is no business of yours."

"But, sir," Jotham cried, "I've lost my father and must find out if he's been here yet. I've not seen him in many weeks and he thinks that I am dead!"

Suddenly the soldier became very interested in Jotham's story. "Your father pays his tax in

Bethlehem?" he asked. When Jotham nodded, the soldier thought for a moment, then said, "Follow me." He pulled Jotham up by the hand and led him through the line of soldiers and over to the milk-white man. The two whispered for a moment, then the milk-white man turned to Jotham and smiled.

"I understand you are looking for your father," he said.

Jotham's heart soared. Soon he would know if his father had been here, and if not, all he had to do was sit and wait for him to show up in one of the three lines. "That is correct, sir," Jotham answered. "If you could just look on your parchments and see if he has been here, I would know how to find him."

The man smiled, and it reminded Jotham of his favorite uncle who always brought him honeycomb. "And is it true that your father thinks you are dead?"

Jotham nodded quickly. "Yes, sir. Many weeks ago I … I was separated from my family, and they think I was killed by a jackal."

"Then your father believes he has one less son than he really does, correct?"

Jotham nodded again. "Yes, sir!" This man is so nice, Jotham thought. He really understands what I'm saying!

"And what is your father's name?" the milk-white man asked, smiling again.

Jotham opened his mouth to answer, but suddenly something about the man's smile made him stop. It was sort of a funny smile, with his lips stretched thin as if the man really wasn't used to smiling at all. It reminded Jotham of something … it reminded him of another smile he'd seen somewhere … it reminded him of … *Decha of Megiddo!*

In an instant Jotham understood. Memories of the man who had been whipped rushed through his mind, and he saw that this would be his father's fate if Jotham gave his name. He recognized now the evil behind the white man's smile, and saw that he was trying to trick Jotham. Jotham wanted to turn and run, but he was surrounded by soldiers that towered over him like Lebanon Cedars. He looked from face to face trying to find a hint of kindness, but there was none. Finally his eyes rested once again on the milk-white man and his crooked little smile.

"Well, boy," the man said, bending down so that his face was inches from Jotham's, "tell me. What is your father's name?"

Consider: Jotham was fooled into trusting the milk-white man—the Roman Procurator—by his pleasant smile. What sort of things are we fooled into believing by the pleasant, but secular, sights and sounds of Christmas?

Part Five

Jotham began to tremble and he felt like he was about to throw up. How could he have been so stupid? He had walked into this trap all on his own, and now he was caught here like a rabbit in a snare. He knew if he told them his father's name, they would search him out. If his father had already paid his taxes they would whip him for not including Jotham in the count of his family. Jotham was quite sure they wouldn't care that his father had no way of knowing he was alive.

"Your father's name, boy!" the milky-white man screamed, no longer smiling. The man's scream was so high he sounded like an animal being butchered, and it scared Jotham so that his legs felt like limp ropes. He could see no escape from these Romans. They were as big as bears with hands as strong as a jackal's jaws. There was nowhere to run and nowhere to hide.

Suddenly Jotham felt one of those jackal-like hands clamp onto the back of his neck. "The Procurator asked you a question, boy!" the soldier roared. Jotham felt tears beginning to form behind his eyes and he wanted to scream. He felt just as hopeless as he had when he was being auctioned off in front of the whole town back in En Gedi.

En Gedi! Nathan!

Suddenly a plan flashed in front of Jotham's eyes and he saw a bit of hope. A wave of fear swept up through his insides at the thought of what would happen if it didn't work, but he knew it was his only chance. He swallowed hard three times and smacked his lips together. Then wrinkling his face into his most pitiful look he stared the milky-white man right in the eye. "Please, sir," he said in his best pleading voice, "do you have a cup of water for a poor leper boy?"

All the fear in Palestine spread across the man's face, and he stumbled backward. The soldier that had clamped his hand around Jotham's neck instantly let go and started yelling and waving his hand through the air. All the other soldiers backed away with looks of fear and disgust, and the three men at the table almost fell over themselves trying to move away.

"Leper!" someone yelled, and suddenly everyone nearby was shouting. The ring of soldiers broke apart, and Jotham saw his chance. Without even thinking about it he ran through the hole in the ring, expecting another hand to clamp around his neck in any second. But the fear of leprosy's slow death kept everyone back, and as Jotham ran, the crowd parted like Moses parting the Red Sea.

"Come back here, you devil," the milky-white man screamed. Jotham looked back only once, and saw that no one was following him. But even so he didn't slow down as he ran through the narrow, winding streets. He had outrun the cries of "leper" now, and the crowds of people thought him just a rude little boy. He was running so fast and thinking so hard that he didn't even notice the donkey Eliakim had given him tied up to a post. Nor did he notice the fat, black-toothed woman that Decha had called "Mother" coming out from a shop.

Finally, panting so hard he thought his lungs would explode, Jotham reached the Inn of Hasrah. He ran inside and slammed the door behind him, leaning against it as if he could keep out the entire Roman Legion all by himself.

"You did not see your family?" Hasrah asked, looking up from where he was repairing a table. Jotham shook his head. "Well, perhaps tomorrow," Hasrah said, returning to his work. "I do not know this Anna you spoke of, but Simeon seems to abide by what she says. Maybe tomorrow I will go with you and speak to the Roman Procurator. He could look on his lists and see if your father has already been here to pay his taxes."

"No," Jotham yelled and shook his head hard.

Hasrah looked at him strangely, but did not pursue the matter, since the inn was full of curious eyes.

Jotham helped Hasrah and his plump little wife feed lamb stew to the many travelers at the inn that night. Every room was full of people, and Jotham wondered where they would all sleep. But after the meal was finished, he watched as they laid sleeping mats all over the floor from wall to wall. Hasrah brought a mat for Jotham and laid it in a corner of the main room, between a fat man who smelled bad and the cool, rough plaster of a wall.

"Before you go to sleep," Hasrah said, "tell me why you cried out at my suggestion to talk to the

Procurator." Now Jotham explained his afternoon adventure to Hasrah. Hasrah laughed heartily, and said that perhaps they shouldn't go see the Procurator after all. He had promised to help Jotham look the next day, and that made Jotham feel good. As he lay down on his mat and covered himself with his scratchy little blanket, he felt as if he was so close to finding his father that he could almost reach out and touch him. Perhaps Hasrah was right, Jotham thought. Perhaps tomorrow he would find his family.

Jotham yawned and pulled the blanket more tightly around his shoulders. It had been a very long day, and it took him only seconds to fall asleep.

Consider: Jotham is excited at being so close to finding his family. Maybe *you're* excited, too, at how close we are to Christmas. It's been a very long wait. What do you think Jotham has learned from his journey? What have *you* discovered in the last few weeks?

Part Six

"Jotham, wake up!" The voice was hissing in his ear, and Jotham swatted at it as if it was an annoying bug. "Jotham, I need your assistance," the voice whispered again, and finally Jotham opened his eyes. He saw Hasrah's face, illuminated by an oil lamp, hovering over him like a ghost in the blackness of the night.

"Wh … what?" Jotham said, rubbing his eyes.

"I need your help, my friend. Some more travelers have arrived—a man and a woman. I tried to send them away, but the woman is about to have a child. I need you to help me clean out the stable again so they may sleep there."

Jotham yawned widely, then climbed out from under his blanket and followed Hasrah, carefully stepping around the sleeping guests. The night air outside the inn was cold, and Jotham gave a little shiver. He was glad that *he* didn't have to sleep in a stable. He followed Hasrah down the little dirt ramp that led to the stable under the inn, passing a rather tall man and a very pregnant woman sitting on a donkey.

Once in the stable, Jotham and Hasrah quickly shooed most of the animals out, then raked out the worst of the dirty hay. "Jotham," Hasrah said at last, "we need some fresh hay for our guests to lie on. Behind the inn is a meadow, and on the far side of the meadow is a small roof covering a stack of hay. Take that cart," he said, pointing to a two-wheeled cart with handles, "and bring back the freshest hay you can find."

Jotham nodded, then left, pulling the little cart behind him. He smiled up at the pregnant woman as he passed her, wondering why she would want to sleep in a stable.

Just as Hasrah had said, the ground sloped downward behind the inn and leveled out into a meadow. Jotham saw that there were many shepherds camped here, their flocks sleeping under the moonlight. Jotham was just starting to form the thought that he should have searched out here for his family, when a voice boomed out of the darkness.

"Who is that?" the man roared. "Who's there!?"

Jotham about jumped out of his skin and gave out a little yell. The man had frightened him so badly he couldn't get his throat to let out any words.

"I said who is there?" the voice demanded again, and now Jotham saw an oil lamp moving toward him, but still he could not speak.

The man was now only a few feet away, and he moved the lamp close to Jotham's face. Then the voice which had been so gruff, became suddenly very soft and amazed. "Jotham," he asked. "Jotham of Jericho? Is that you?"

The lamp moved away from Jotham's eyes then, and the face he saw before him sent lightning through his body. "Eliakim!" he yelled, and clamped his arms around his old friend's legs.

Eliakim hugged the boy tightly. "It is good to see you," he said. "I was afraid we would not find you again."

Consider: Jotham walked right past Mary, the mother of the Messiah, and didn't even know it. If *you're* not careful, you could pass right by the Messiah this Christmas without even knowing it. What can you do to prevent this happening?

Part Seven

Just then another familiar voice came out of the dark. "Jotham?"

Jotham turned and saw Tabitha walking toward him. "Tabitha," he yelled, and almost felt as if he was home again. Tabitha didn't say anything more, but turned and ran away. Jotham was confused by this, but turned back to Eliakim. "Have you seen my father?" he asked.

"Sadly no, little one," Eliakim answered. "But then, I do not know him so I could very well pass him on the road and not realize it."

Tabitha returned then, carrying in front of her a loaf of bread. "I baked for you every day," she whispered. "Just like I promised."

Tears came to Jotham's eyes and he said, "My mind would not forget you either!"

Then Tabitha started talking about how much she had missed Jotham and about all the things that had happened since she saw him last. But Jotham only heard a few words because, behind her across the field, standing by a fire with his back to Jotham, was a man—a man that looked terribly familiar. Jotham watched the man, silouhetted against the fire, for several moments. Then, right in the middle of Tabitha's talking, he walked around her.

"Jotham?" Tabitha said. "Jotham! Where are you going?"

But Jotham didn't answer. He started across the field, slowly at first, not taking his eyes off the man. Then he began to walk faster, and finally broke into a run as he became more certain.

"Father!" he yelled at last. "Father!"

The man turned, and Jotham saw that it was indeed his father. A curious look crossed his father's face, then shock, then joy. "Jotham?" he asked breathlessly. "Jotham!" he yelled and started running toward his son.

Tears of joy began to flow down Jotham's cheeks as he realized his long ordeal was finally over. In a moment he would be in his father's arms and would never leave them again.

But then, when father and son were about thirty paces apart, a dark shadow swooped out from a stand of olive trees.

It was Decha of Megiddo.

In one smooth motion Decha landed between Jotham and his father and drew his long, curved sword. In the same instant two of his henchmen grabbed Jotham's father and quickly bound him with ropes on each wrist. Eliakim and his brother caught up with Jotham and skidded to a stop beside him.

"Stay back, devil!" Decha roared at Jotham. "Or your father will visit his ancestors a bit sooner than I had planned!"

"Stay back, Jotham," his father yelled. "My brother speaks no empty threats!"

"Your *brother!*" Jotham gasped.

"*Half* brother," Jotham's father, Asa, corrected.

"Yes, now," Decha said as he threatened Asa's neck with the point of his sword, "that does seem to be the problem, doesn't it?"

"What do you want, Decha?" Asa spat.

"Only what is rightfully mine! Only my *birthright!* The flocks and tents and camels of our father!"

"Rightfully *yours!*" Asa said in disbelief. "Of all our brothers you are the *last* who should receive our father's inheritance!" Then he turned to Jotham and explained. "Decha killed our father when we were just boys."

"The man beat me and denied me food!" Decha screamed.

"He did no such thing," Asa answered. "He was the kindest and most gentle father a boy could have. You've been telling that lie so long you're starting to believe it!"

Decha instantly calmed and drew his sword back, testing its edge with his thumb. "Perhaps," he said calmly. "But the fact remains that I am the firstborn of Joseph and I deserve to have his wealth."

"Yes, you are the firstborn of his first wife and I am the firstborn of his *second* wife," Asa said slowly. "But my mother bore me long before yours bore you, and the law clearly gives *me* our father's inheritance."

Decha sighed. "Which is why, brother, I must now kill you. And then I will kill all my other half brothers," he moved close to Asa and put the sword at his throat once more, "including the youngest, who even now waits in a stable up in Bethlehem."

Asa shook his head slowly. "Why, Decha? What did anyone ever do to you to fill you with such hate?"

"That's simple," Decha whispered, and the stench of his breath made Asa gag. "Our father loved you and your mother more than me and my mother."

"That's a lie, Decha," Asa said. "Our father showed your mother every kindness. But she rewarded him with jealousy."

Decha stared at Asa for a moment, and Jotham felt as if his uncle was the devil himself.

"I should have killed you when I killed our father," Decha said. Then he took a long step back and raised his sword over his head. "Goodbye, brother."

"No!" Jotham screamed, but was helpless to stop his uncle. Decha took one last look at Jotham and grinned his black-toothed, rotting grin. Then he started to swing the sword at Asa.

And that's when the cry went up from the woods.

It was a high-pitched wail that sounded like the squawk of a peacock. Everyone turned and looked. A moment later a blurry figure sprang from the woods, did three cartwheels, and landed right in front of Decha.

"Nathan!" Jotham yelled with a grin.

Nathan tweaked Decha on the nose. "Are we being a naughty boy?" he asked, like a parent.

Decha roared in anger and swung his sword at Nathan, but Nathan, once again acting the part of the fool, dropped below the blade and did a back flip, landing on the ground ten feet away as if he were lounging on his bedroll. "Temper, temper!" Nathan chided. Decha screamed again and went after Nathan, but Nathan was too quick. He spun around twice, then dove between the legs of one of the henchmen.

"I'll kill you both!" Decha roared, and started after Nathan. But once again Nathan jumped up, spun, and sprang, this time ending up behind one of the henchmen. Then Nathan did another back flip in such a way that he ended up standing just inches in front of Decha. The shocked Decha just stared at him with wide eyes.

"Now, now," Nathan said, "we mustn't play with big knives!" And with that Nathan plucked the sword right out of Decha's hand. With three more flips he ended up back at the edge of the woods, the weaponless Decha looking down at his hands in disbelief.

Jotham and Eliakim's clan cheered and laughed, then started toward Decha and his henchmen. The henchmen grew scared and almost dropped the ropes that held Asa. But then Jotham watched in horror as a noose on the end of a rope came flying out of the woods and dropped around Nathan's neck. With a laugh and a cackle, Decha's mother rode out of the woods on the donkey she had stolen from Jotham. She was holding the rope and pulling it tight. Nathan dropped the sword and grabbed the rope around his neck, choking. In a flash, Decha swooped up the sword and threatened Asa's neck with it once more.

"Stay back, all of you!" he yelled, and Jotham and his group stopped short. "Very well then," Decha hissed, looking at Nathan, "I shall have one more head to decorate my tent!"

He turned back to Jotham and said, "Wait right there, boy. You're next!"

With that he raised his sword once again and Jotham screamed. Nathan pulled the rope away from his throat just enough to get a breath. Looking at Jotham he yelled, "David!" Jotham was so mixed up and scared he felt as if his head was full of fog. Dazed, he turned to look at Nathan, not understanding what his friend was yelling. "David!" Nathan yelled again.

And suddenly, the fog went away.

In one smooth motion Jotham swept a stone up off the ground and slid his sling out of his belt. Even as he raised the sling over his head he was putting the stone into its leather pouch. With three mighty turns of his arm Jotham spun the sling overhead. Then, looking straight at Decha, he let go.

Decha was in his backswing now, the hate and anger of a lifetime going into this one swing of his sword. As he tried to put all his might into this one moment, he swung the sword behind him, turning away from Asa. And in that moment his eyes grew wide and the blood drained from his face as he saw hurling toward his forehead the rock from Jotham's sling.

A moment later the stone hit Decha between the eyes, and Decha dropped dead.